BACK TO K

BACK TO WORK
THE STORY OF PWA

THE MACMILLAN COMPANY
NEW YORK · BOSTON · CHICAGO · DALLAS
ATLANTA · SAN FRANCISCO

MACMILLAN & CO., LIMITED
LONDON · BOMBAY · CALCUTTA
MELBOURNE

THE MACMILLAN COMPANY
OF CANADA, LIMITED
TORONTO

This is not a mural, but a picture of men working on a typical sewer tunnel under a busy Chicago thoroughfare. This immense sewage disposal project, the largest of its kind in the world, is financed with an allotment of $42,000,000 from the Public Works Administration.

BACK TO WORK

THE STORY OF PWA

BY

HAROLD L. ICKES

SECRETARY OF THE INTERIOR
AND
ADMINISTRATOR OF PUBLIC WORKS

NEW YORK
THE MACMILLAN COMPANY
1935

TO

FRANKLIN DELANO ROOSEVELT
President of the United States

PREFACE

In order to correct the ills of unemployment and again to start the wheels of industry, the national administration, in midsummer of 1933, under power granted to it by Congress, undertook a program of public works. PWA, as this enterprise soon came to be known after our American fashion of familiar abbreviations, has aroused and held the interest of the people in every part of the land. So far-flung have been its activities that there are few sections of the country where visible evidence of PWA may not be seen by the interested. In hundreds of thousands of homes PWA has meant steady wages, which in their turn have meant food and shelter and clothing, with perhaps a bit left over for some of the comforts and modest luxuries of life.

By the terms of the original National Industrial Recovery Act, PWA was due to expire by limitation of law on June 16, 1935. By a recent act of Congress its life has been extended to July 1, 1937. As a result the activities of PWA will be continued and expanded as part of the recovery program to be financed out of the 4 billion 880 million dollars recently appropriated by the Works Relief Resolution.

In the circumstances it seems appropriate to render to the people some general accounting of what PWA has done and been during the almost two years of its existence and to give some indication of what it may be able to do during the next two years on the basis of the wider experience, the better technique and the broader vision that it has acquired during its short, but eventful, life. In the pages of this book, therefore, I am trying, in broad outline, to tell the people, whose money it was, what became of the 3 billion 300 million dollars appropriated in the National Industrial Recovery Act of 1933, and the 400 million dollars additional allocated by the President to PWA out of the sums appropriated in the Emergency Deficiency Bill of 1934.

As the one entrusted by the President with the grave responsibility of administering this huge total sum of 3 billion 700 million dollars, I want to say that whatever success has attended that administration has been due to the guidance and inspiration of the President. His has been the vision that has never dimmed. Franklin D. Roosevelt will be written down in history not only as the world's greatest builder; he will likewise be known for all time to come as the greatest planner. I never cease to marvel at the understanding grasp that the President at all times has had of the most obscure and detailed items in connection with a vast program that already has comprehended almost 20,000 projects in practically every county in the United States and which has reached also into our outlying possessions.

To the members of the staff of PWA I take this occasion to express my admiration and gratitude. They have functioned in most trying circumstances. They have given of their time and abilities freely and unstintingly. If they have ever kept their eyes on the clock it has been in order that they might not be late at their desks; closing time day after day has been that hour of the day or night when there was no further task presently to be performed or when they had reached the limit of their physical endurance. They have been a fine and admirable group, with whom it has been not only a pleasure but a real distinction to be associated.

I would have the members of the PWA staff know that I realize that to them is due the credit for a record of accomplishment in an unexplored field with which both they and the country have the right to feel satisfied. I wish to express particular appreciation to the many members of my staff who have generously contributed suggestions and time to this book, especially Mr. Michael W. Straus and Dr. Clark Foreman and their associates, Mr. Jonathan W. Latimer, Mr. Michael Ross and Mr. Joel David Wolfsohn.

HAROLD L. ICKES.

Washington,
May 15, 1935.

CONTENTS

ILLUSTRATIONS

BACK TO WORK
THE STORY OF PWA

CHAPTER I

NO HELP WANTED

AROUND a polished, oval-shaped table in the office of the Secretary of the Interior, four days past the middle of June of 1933, sat nine men. Although it was an hour short of noon, Washington already sweltered in yellow sunlight so oppressive that even within the spacious room rising currents of hot, damp air had forced some of the men to shed their coats. Informally attired, they sat on the edge of their leather-cushioned chairs, their faces alert, eager to begin work despite the heat.

They had met to plan the expenditure of the greatest sum of money ever raised by a nation for a peace-time purpose. The group was the Special Board of Public Works and I, as Secretary of the Interior, was to preside over it until the sum of three billion three hundred million dollars, appropriated by Congress for an emergency public works program, had been well spent.

All of us realized there was plenty of work in store, work of primary importance to the Nation. I remember my own feeling of bewilderment when the President, following the Cabinet meeting two days before, had informed me I was to be chairman of the newly created Special Board. But the warm glow of pride engendered by this expression of his confidence in me was considerably tempered by a hollow feeling that the responsibility was a thousand times greater than I had ever before carried.

This confusion of sensations, which certainly must have been shared by the others on the Special Board, was aggravated by a realization that there was no precedent for what we had to do, since never before had there been a construction program on such a scale. My mind, as we prepared to hold our first meeting, ran back over the history of public works in America, over the events, political and economic, which had led to the birth of the present program.

. . . . .

The great buildings of the past that have come down to us as monuments of enterprise and genius to spur us on also to achieve worth-while things in stone and steel and cement were, generally speaking, public buildings. The labor employed on them was slave labor or serf labor, the former kept to his task by the lash and the latter by the moral superiority of his overlord and the control by that overlord of the serf's meager means of livelihood.

Here in America it has also been true that many of our outstanding structures, monumental buildings, dams, bridges and mountain-penetrating roads—all marvels of engineering skill—have been paid for out of the public purse. Yet such public construction in this comparatively new country has been insignificant as compared with the building done by private enterprise. Our schools, roads and public hospitals, our monuments and governmental buildings have been tremendously important economic and social factors in our national life. They have utilized, however, only a small portion of the labor, material and capital employed in the construction industry, which is second in importance in the United States only to agriculture. The national expenditures on construction from 1926 to 1929 reached the impressive figure of twelve billion dollars a year. Three-quarters of this sum was spent by private interests. Probably no nation in all the history of the world, even on a comparable population basis, has ever spent so much money year after year as was being expended in the United States on construction projects immediately prior to the economic crash in 1929.

When it comes to labor, the contrast with other countries and other periods is even more startling. Our labor has been free labor, drawn from among the finest of our citizens. Not only has it been free, but it was paid higher wages, during the period of great building activity prior to 1929, than labor has ever earned in any country in the world, ancient or modern. About three millions of well-paid Americans were employed directly on construction, while it is estimated that at least as many more were earning good wages for producing and transporting the required materials.

This fine economic process, so necessary to the happiness and well-being of those supported by it, was involved in the break-up of 1929. There is no need to record in detail the losses suffered by the private construction industry as the result of the depression. It is enough to know that in 1933 the former torrent of construction expenditures had become a mere trickle of three billion dollars, only half of which was accounted for by private construction. This huge dislocation added greatly to the growing problem of unemployment. The country found itself in a condition of want in the midst of potential plenty.

President Roosevelt, while governor of New York and honorary president of the American Construction Council, was one of the first to comment publicly on the anomalous situation which showed, on one hand, relief rolls crowded with the names of building-trade workers, and yards and warehouses filled with lumber, steel and cement; and, on the other, communities with insanitary housing, inadequate sewer systems and unsatisfactory roads. He saw the necessity for a new social objective if prosperity was to be restored and the feet of the people once more set on the road toward a happier and fuller life. As early as 1930 he said:

"It is high time that every community lay down a definite program or plan looking toward the elimination of living conditions that do not come up to the standard of modern times. I hope the American Construction Council will be able to arouse the interest and the co-operation of the executives of all the cities in the country, large and small, for it goes almost without saying that no city can boast of conditions which do not need to be improved."

This odd conjunction of idle labor and unused material with a desperate need for further public works was forcibly called to the attention of the nation by the relief situation. This had become so heavy that local funds were becoming exhausted in many localities and the burden of maintaining the unemployed was being thrust upon the Federal Government. The question arose over the best method of taking care of the millions who desired work but could not find it. Students of the depression began to declare that, so long as private enterprise was unable to employ those on relief, the government should take up the slack by putting people to work on useful public projects which at the same time would raise the social standards of the country. They pointed out that roads, schools, sewers and water systems, bridges, slum-clearance projects and public buildings of all kinds would provide a broad field for construction activity. The wages paid to the workers would also revive private industry.

Back of this obviously simple solution for a critical situation lay a history of persistent struggling against an antiquated and apparently impregnable point of view, clung to tenaciously by the Hoover administration. My mind irresistibly goes back, in this connection, to a meeting I attended in Washington on March 11, 1931. This was one of the first occasions upon which public works and economic planning were intelligently discussed.

The meeting was called by a group of five senators, George W. Norris, of Nebraska; Edward P. Costigan, of Colorado; the late Bronson Cutting, of New Mexico; Robert M. LaFollette, Jr., of Wisconsin; and Burton K. Wheeler, of Montana, and was attended by forward-looking public men and socially minded thinkers from all quarters of the United States. The statement outlining the objects of the meeting said:

"In the midst of depression, the Nation is without effective political or economic leadership. We believe that a constructive solution for problems can be found by men and women who are aligned with different political parties. To this end, it is our purpose that the conference shall be non-partisan in character, and shall be devoted to the exchange of ideas looking solely to the formulation of a sound legislative program to be advanced at the next session of Congress."

At this conference, Senator LaFollette made a report for a committee on unemployment and industrial stabilization. This called for "the full use of the resources at the command of Federal, State and local governments to deal with the problem of unemployment," and pointed out that "the creation of a coördinated national system of employment exchanges would now be under way if it had not been for the unjustifiable veto of the Wagner Bill." A subcommittee was appointed to study the "place of public works in industrial stabilization."

Most of the measures advocated at this conference had to wait until March 4, 1933, before there was an administration in Washington with enough courage and vision to take the steps necessary to revive the country. Many of those who took part in the deliberations are now to be found associated with the Roosevelt administration, engaged in working out steps delayed altogether too long. Senators LaFollette and Costigan, who kept hammering away in Congress in the pre-Roosevelt days for an extensive public works program to relieve the distress of the unemployed, had a large share in bringing about the change in public opinion which eventually occurred.

It is important to emphasize the part played by President Roosevelt in uniting and leading sentiment for a development of public works. From the governor's mansion in Albany he sent an understanding telegram to the

group which met in Washington. Long before that, as
president of the Construction Council, which he helped
to organize, he had been an active advocate of better
homes and slum clearance. It was natural then, when it
seemed clear that the unemployment problem must be
attacked by way of public construction, that President
Roosevelt should summon to the White House for con-
sultation those groups which had been working toward a
similar goal.

On May 1, 1933, when all the Nation was anxiously
waiting to see what would be done to check the depression, Dwight L. Hoopingarner, secretary of the Council,
said:

"The latest steps in this movement are the crystalliza-
tion of plans advocated by Franklin D. Roosevelt for
many years when he was president of the American Construction Council, as witnessed for example, by the national movement on slum clearance inaugurated within a
few months after the onslaught of the depression in 1929.
This movement for public works will furnish a program
of increasing employment over a period of years on a
progressively developed and balanced scale."

During this period another man who was insistent upon
action by the national government was Senator Robert F.
Wagner of New York. He began his campaign for public
works early in 1928, when he introduced in the United
States Senate bills for a reliable census of the unemployed;
for the creation of a Federal Employment Stabilization
Board to plan public works years ahead of their need, and
for the creation of a Federal Employment Agency System
to provide for the shifting of surplus labor to places of

labor scarcity. His proposal for the collection of labor statistics became law in 1930 and his stabilization plan went into the statute books in 1931.

As the depression became worse, Senator Wagner plunged into the problem of emergency relief. He participated actively in framing the law which created the Reconstruction Finance Corporation in January of 1932. Later in the same session he introduced the Emergency Relief and Construction Act which was incontinently vetoed by President Hoover. However, after compromises which limited its scope to self-liquidating projects, a greatly modified bill finally became law. This act provided 373 million dollars for Federal construction and 300 million for relief loans to States, while increasing the funds of the RFC by one and one-half billion dollars for self-liquidating construction work. Senator Wagner continued his fight in 1933 and joined in sponsoring an amendment to the 1932 act which increased by 500 million dollars the amount of Federal funds available for unemployment relief.

With the deepening of the depression and with the development of more terrible and frequent symptoms of unemployment--the apple salesmen, the breadliners, the beggars, the half-starved wandering children, the emaciated hitch-hikers, the tragic and futile riots—more apparent each day, the chorus of voices favoring public works grew in volume. The members of this chorus were a strange assortment of economists and theorists, of business and professional men, of politicians and private citizens, of Democrats, Republicans and Socialists. For a time even Herbert Hoover, as Secretary of Commerce, had in theory favored a program of public works to fill in such an economic void, but when he became President and an acute need arose to embody this fine idea in living form, the plan was allowed to precede him into oblivion. In the meantime, however, able though diversely interested men became advocates of a construction program.

In June of 1931 Norman Thomas, the Socialist candidate for the Presidency, announced that he was in favor of a five billion dollar bond issue for public construction. Thirteen months later an appropriation of two billions, three hundred millions of dollars for public works was advocated by Senator Joseph T. Robinson of Arkansas and this proposal was endorsed by Alfred E. Smith, Owen D. Young and Bernard M. Baruch.

In 1932 Senators LaFollette and Costigan introduced and fought for a bill for five and one-half billion dollars for public works. In August of that year the Advertising Club of New York went on record for a four billion dollar fund in language very like that employed in an earlier appeal from twenty-eight American mayors for a five billion dollar appropriation. In June, William Green, president of the American Federation of Labor, had asked for an identical sum. Others who came forward during this period with public works plans included Gerard Swope, Fred I. Kent, M. C. Rorty, Henry S. Dennison and Henry I. Harriman.

While all these people and some others who were urging the proposition of public works as a theory of economics were personally out of touch with the urgent reality of gnawing starvation and want, their position was supported by many victims of unemployment. A vivid picture of the times was painted before a Senate committee considering an amendment to the Relief and Construction Act of 1932 by persons who had seen the whites of the eyes of want and despair and broken morale. An effective witness at this hearing, which was held in February of 1933, was Sidney M. Smoot, who had been out of work since 1929. Here is a vignette of his testimony under the questioning of the senators:

Senator Brookhart: You are one of the destitute men in the city?

Mr. Smoot: Yes, I just want to speak along the line that we are up against it, all the single men. I am a widower.

Senator Brookhart: You have no relief of any kind?

Mr. Smoot: No, sir. We have been to relief boards, and they all say "Nothing for single men."

Senator Brookhart: And you cannot get work?

Mr. Smoot: No, there is no work to be got. I have been in construction work all my life—for twenty-three years.

Senator Wagner: How do you get along now?

Mr. Smoot: Well, one of the colored men went over to the relief and got us a bag of turnips. And we ask restaurants, hotels and good housewives for eats.

Senator Brookhart: These men like you, would they work if they could get jobs?

Mr. Smoot: Well, certainly; every one of them would. The majority of them worked in the relief last winter, but this year there was nothing provided for single men.

Another witness was Edward F. McGrady, representing the American Federation of Labor, who later became Assistant Secretary of Labor under President Roosevelt.

Mr. McGrady: Our records show that there are 12,000,000 out of work and in addition about 9,000,000 only getting part-time work.

Senator Brookhart: How many dependents do you figure the 12,000,000 would have?

Mr. McGrady: We figure that in the United States today there are no less than 45,000,000 people living in poverty. As to living conditions we sent out investigators and found sixteen people living in four rooms. Two, three and four families have combined, and are living in one house. Children everywhere are suffering from malnutrition. We have found in our organization that working men who have been idle for 12, 14 or 16 months, and who are given an opportunity to return to their old employment, cannot stand the hours of labor on account of undernourishment. The relief necessity is increasing greater than unemployment; the need is going to be greater because their own resources are becoming exhausted. In October, 1932, for instance, unemployment increased 60.5 per cent but families aided increased 94.5 per cent. There will be adequate relief or there will be rebellion.

One of the last witnesses was Col. John P. Hogan, chairman of the Committee on Public Works of the American Society of Civil Engineers, who put the case for public works before the committee in this fashion:

"Money expended in doles or direct relief contributes little to the stimulation of trade, whereas money spent in public works stimulates business not only in the community itself but throughout the material and transportation industries. Owing to the very natural desire to escape the tax burden, during the past year we have followed a policy directly counter to sound economy by greatly reducing or suspending our State and municipal public works and thus adding vast numbers to the already great army of unemployed.

"Public works built at the present low wage and price levels and financed at reasonable rates of interest will carry a very low cost. It is good business as well as good tactics to use this opportunity to add substantially to the public wealth."

All of these demands, which had fallen upon the deaf ears of the preceding administration, no longer went unheeded after President Roosevelt was inaugurated. On March 11, 1933, he conferred with the three musketeers of the long public works struggle, Senators Costigan, Wagner and LaFollette, discussing with them the establishment of camps for the unemployed and the making of RFC loans for public works. Secretary of Labor Frances Perkins later was invited to enter the discussions and on May 7, in a radio talk, the President disclosed his intention of asking Congress to pass the legislation which later became known as the National Industrial Recovery Act.

Some time prior to this address the work of drafting a recovery bill had been started independently by various groups. Some were working on codes for industry, while others occupied themselves with public works alone. The fact that the two ideas were coupled together in one bill was due entirely to the President. It had been agreed by his confidential advisers during the campaign that public works had to be combined with some supporting plan to supply a firm industrial base through wage and hour agreements. But when the different groups went to the White House to say that they were unable to weld the two ideas together, the President waved them away, saying, in effect: "Don't come back until you get together."

Dr. Raymond Moley, who had been one of those most active in the earlier "inner circle" conferences, talked to Senator Wagner of the necessity for combining the two theories. Although the New York senator had interested himself primarily in a public works program he saw the logical connection between them. PWA was to entice the Nation back to a normal status by starting the flow of money through wages and the purchase of materials and NRA was to provide the machinery for keeping it there.

In the meantime, Dr. Moley had called in General Hugh S. Johnson to look over the many plans that had been submitted for the control of industry. Already labor, by means of the Black Bill, was trying to spread work by limiting employment to thirty hours a week. Secretary of Labor Perkins had attempted to put teeth in this bill by suggesting a minimum wage provision, but the idea was greeted with cries of "Dictatorship," "Sovietism" and "Radicalism" from employers everywhere. Miss Perkins was astonished at the tumult her "modest proposal" caused. There were other plans, a multiplicity of them. All of these General Johnson took to a hotel room in Washington, carefully locking the door behind him.

Twenty-four hours later he appeared with a two-page

rough draft of a bill. It appeared that his idea, too, was to combine a public works program with a plan for a lifting of wages and a reduction of working hours by industry. Industry was to be forced into line by a blanket rule. General Johnson was impressed with the necessity for speed. The thing had to be done immediately, he insisted; there was no time for business, through the trade associations, to prepare codes. His theory was to blanket all business and industry under a code; then, if anyone was hurt too severely, perhaps an exception could later be made.

His views were somewhat modified by others engaged in working on the bill. Finally, after he, Senator Wagner and Donald R. Richberg had held many discussions, the National Industrial Recovery Act was ready for the President's inspection. It was then that chance played its part in the proceedings. The final copy of the bill had been drafted by Simon H. Rifkind, then Senator Wagner's secretary, and Senator Wagner was looking it over. The office was crowded, with much conversation going on. It is reported that Senator Wagner called out to Rifkind: "Does the three billion for public works include the three hundred million for New York?"

Above the din, Wagner thought he heard Rifkind say, "Put it in." Actually, Rifkind said, "I put it in," but Wagner crossed out the figure $3,000,000,000 and wrote in $3,300,000,000. Then he hurried over to the White House to tell the President that this figure represented what his group believed it would be necessary to spend in order to "prime the pump" of business.

On May 17 the President sent his eagerly awaited message to Congress. A sentence of it read: "Before the special session of Congress adjourns, I recommend two further steps in our national campaign to put people to work." One of these steps was to be known later as the NRA; the other was a proposal to give the Executive "full power to start a large program of direct employment." In the message the President also said he felt sure "that approximately $3,300,000,000 can be invested in useful and necessary public construction, and at the same time put the largest number of people to work. . . ."

In both Houses of Congress, bills already drafted were introduced to give effect to the President's recommendations. Congressman Doughton presented one—designated as HR 5755 in the House, and Senator Wagner asked the Senate for unanimous consent to introduce a similar bill. Immediately heated debate arose over the proposed measures. One congressman, in a forty-minute address, insisted the whole idea was directly opposed to "the spirit of Valley Forge." Bare feet, leaving bloody footprints on frozen ground, appeared to him to be heroic even if unnecessary. Mr. Beck of Pennsylvania opposed the bill in the House with profound constitutional arguments supported by lengthy quotations from Jonathan Swift's *Tale of a Tub*. Most of the opposition, however, was directed at the first title of the bill setting up the NRA. So heavy for a time was the bombardment that it was even proposed that Title I be dropped and the bill limited to the public works program provided for in Title II. The essential link between the two sections was seen in the end by most of the debaters. Mr. Kelly of Pennsylvania pointed out: "There is power in the public works title to turn over the wheel, and there is power enough in the industrial recovery title to keep it turning."

Under a special rule, debate in the Lower House was limited to seven hours and the measure passed on May 26 by a vote of 323 to 76. The Senate was in the agonies of gestation for a longer period. Not only did his colleagues receive jabs from Senator Wagner and others ardently supporting the bill, they were constantly being pricked by their constituents. Even Senator Fess of Ohio was forced to admit, in a peroration concluding his argument against the bill, that "I have simply been amazed at the urgent messages which have come to me, not only from my own State, but from other parts of the Nation urging me to support this legislation . . . from the highest-minded business men . . . from the most progressive and aggressive labor organizations . . ."

On June 12, three days before Congress adjourned, the Senate passed the bill 57-24. It was signed on June 16 by President Roosevelt. Just a month had elapsed since he had sent his message to Congress.

In the meantime, while Congress was earnestly debating, the President, in anticipation of its passage, requested General Johnson to set up an organization for the administration of the Act. He asked the General, who had a reputation for quick action, to assemble the machinery of administration with all possible speed so that only a pressure on the starter would be needed to set it in motion after the bill had received legislative approval. He advised Johnson to assemble this machinery with the idea in mind that some one else might be named administrator.

General Johnson at once centered his attention on Title

I of the Act—to be known later as the NRA—because he foresaw that this would meet with the most opposition. Under Title II—the public works program—he asked Colonel George R. Spalding of the army engineers, whom he had known and admired during the World War, to take over the job of organization. Since he was acting without formal authority, Colonel Spalding had to proceed under difficulties. One of his chief troubles was his inability to offer permanent positions to members of his hastily assembled staff. He was unable to offer temporary salaries, or even expenses, to his assistants. Yet, despite these handicaps, which in the organization of a private corporation would have proved insurmountable, he managed to gather around himself a group of able men. Many of them were engineers furnished by the War Department, which regarded the public works program with enthusiasm, and practically all of the others came from organizations that had sponsored and fought for the public works bill.

Second in command of the unofficial PWA was Colonel Henry M. Waite, a vice-president of the American Society of Civil Engineers, recommended to Colonel Spalding by that society. Colonel Waite's career as a municipal administrator, engineer and transportation executive marked him as an exceptional man. He had been city manager of Dayton, Ohio, for nearly four years at a time when this form of city government was regarded as dubiously experimental and before that he had been chief engineer for the city of Cincinnati. During the war his capacity was recognized by the post given to him of Deputy General Director of Transportation with the American Expeditionary Forces in France. His last undertaking had been the construction of the great forty million dollar Union Terminal in Cincinnati. He had completed this project in 1933, six months ahead of the original schedule, and within the estimated cost.

When Colonel Waite arrived in Washington he was informed by Colonel Spalding of the extremely ephemeral possibilities of the job.

"We may be thrown out of this thing at any time," Colonel Spalding said, "or one of us may be called upon to act as the Administrator. I think we ought to agree now to forget who is supposed to be boss and work in coöperation."

Colonel Waite agreed that no matter which of them might be placed in charge of the program after it had been approved by Congress, or even if some one else were made Administrator, they would coöperate.

Two of the other important army men to join the growing staff were Major Philip B. Fleming and Major Robert W. Crawford. Robert D. Kohn, former president of the American Institute of Architects and connected with the Construction League, volunteered his services, as did Francis M. Knight of the Continental-Illinois National Bank of Chicago, and Colonel John P. Hogan. At the suggestion of Colonel Waite, Henry T. Hunt, a former mayor of Cincinnati and then practicing law in New York, was selected as acting legal counsel.

This group faced a tremendous job. Never before in any country had an organization similar to theirs been formed. They had nothing to go upon; no precedent, no set of rules upon which to model their plans. Moreover, they were not even an official body. To add to the difficulties, Congress was still in the process of modifying and perfecting the bill. Each change in the National Industrial Recovery Act meant a corresponding change in the set-up of the temporary organization.

One of the chief changes was the enlargement of Section 202 of the Act, dealing with the kinds of projects on which the money might be spent, to include a number of categories not in the original bill. "Flood control, river and drainage improvements as recommended by the army engineers," and "construction of low-cost housing" were amplified to include "reconstruction, alteration and repair." Also such projects as "hospitals, reservoirs, pumping plants and dry-docks" were brought into the section.

To add to the general confusion, the offices in the Department of Commerce were being flooded with requests for funds for special projects. Nothing was too big, or too small for which to ask. A mayor in the Middle West wanted to redecorate his office; a telegram from a promoter urged the construction, at a cost of twenty billion dollars, of a moving road, something like an escalator, from New York to San Francisco, along which were to be built drug stores, theaters, churches, etc.; a preacher in Kansas wanted money to buy Bibles for his congregation. The mail grew larger each day.

Despite the overwhelming task and the constant interruptions, the group managed to work out a plan. The organization was to be decentralized, each State having its own engineer and administrator, but subject to a headquarters at Washington. Lists of names of men equipped to act as State engineers were supplied by the American Society of Civil Engineers and telegrams notifying those selected of their appointment were prepared so they could be sent out when the law was finally signed. A circular was prepared by Mr. Hunt, giving information which would be needed by applicants. These were actually sent out with application forms by air mail before the National Industrial Recovery Act had emerged from Congress. Everything was done to facilitate the use of the money as soon as it should be appropriated. The idea was speed, more speed. There was even under consideration the establishment of a teletype system between Washington and the forty-eight State headquarters.

On June 16, the President issued his executive order authorizing the expenditure of the 3 billion 300 million dollars and named Colonel Donald H. Sawyer, chairman of the Federal Employment Stabilization Board, as Temporary Administrator of the Act. This order read:

ADMINISTRATION OF PUBLIC WORK

Pursuant to the authority of "An ACT to encourage national industrial recovery, to foster fair competition, and to provide for the construction of certain useful public works, and for other purposes," approved June 16, 1933, and in order to effectuate Title II—Public Works and Construction Projects—thereof:

1. I hereby appoint Colonel Donald H. Sawyer to exercise temporarily the office of Federal Emergency Administrator of Public Works.

I hereby appoint a *Special Board for Public Works* consisting of the following:

The Secretary of the Interior, Chairman; the Secretary of War; the Attorney General; the Secretary of Agriculture; the Secretary of Commerce; the Secretary of Labor; the Director of the Budget;

Colonel George R. Spalding and Assistant Secretary of the Treasury Robert.

During the ensuing 30 days the Federal Emergency Administrator of Public Works shall have authority to allot the sum of not to exceed $400,000,000 provided for in Title II of said Act for highway building for distribution among the States, Territories, and the District of Columbia, and authority to allot the sum of not to exceed $238,000,000 to the Department of the Navy for the construction of certain vessels, the construction whereof conforms to the London Naval Treaty, and has heretofore been approved by me.

The distribution of the money herein allocated for public roads shall be subject to the approval of the Board for Public Works.

The Federal Emergency Administrator of Public Works is hereby authorized to employ such necessary personnel on a temporary basis as may be approved by the Board.

During the next 20 days it shall be the duty of the Federal Emergency Administrator of Public Works and the Board herein constituted to study and report to me on all public works projects which have heretofore been submitted or shall hereafter be submitted.

(Signed) FRANKLIN D. ROOSEVELT.

.　　　.　　　.　　　.

So we return to that first meeting of the Special Board in my unpleasantly warm office in the Interior Building. Certain broad policies had been outlined by the Act, but actually we were responsible, subject only to the President, for the manner in which the money was to be spent. The second title of the law provided that the program could include construction, repair and improvement of public highways and parkways, public buildings, and any publicly owned instrumentalities and facilities; the conservation and development of natural resources, including water works, flood control and river and harbor improvements. It was decided that as a matter of law this category included railroad maintenance and equipment. Another important provision was one authorizing low-cost housing and slum-clearance projects.

Authority to distribute the funds was vested in the President. The bill authorized him to undertake construction directly, or to finance construction by loans to States, municipalities and other public bodies and to certain private corporations. He was further authorized to make outright grants to States and other public bodies of not to exceed 30 per cent of the cost of labor and materials of a project, with loans of 70 per cent to be protected by "reasonable security." The bill also provided that the money should be used to give the maximum amount of employment at an adequate level of wages.*

These instructions, coupled with those in the President's executive order, were our only guideposts. Actually we had the broadest powers imaginable. It was up to us to formulate policies for the allotment of the money and then to oversee its distribution. We knew we had for expenditure an enormous sum, but we had no intimation of the difficulties which quickly arose to plague us like a swarm of locusts.

* For the complete Title II of the NIRA, see Appendix A.

CHAPTER II

THREE BILLIONS TO SPEND

THE National Industrial Recovery Act earmarked the sum of 400 million dollars for roads on the same basis of apportionment between the States as Federal aid for roads had been granted in the past. In his executive order the President authorized the Administrator to allot not to exceed this sum for the purpose stated, and the same order carried the further authority to allot not to exceed 238 million dollars to the navy for the construction of certain vessels. At the first meeting of the Special Board for Public Works these allocations were made a matter of formal record. Present at this meeting, at which the Secretary of the Interior, designated as chairman, presided, were Secretary of War George H. Dern, Assistant Secretary of Agriculture Rexford G. Tugwell, Attorney General Homer S. Cummings, Secretary of Commerce Daniel C. Roper; Turner W. Battle, assistant to the Secretary of Labor; Colonel Spalding; Assistant Secretary of the Treasury Robert; Solicitor General Biggs; R. O. Kloeber, representing the Bureau of the Budget, and Colonel Sawyer.

During the first months, Secretary Dern attended Board meetings regularly, but occasionally he was represented by Assistant Secretary Harry H. Woodring. Later, Major General Robert E. Callan, assistant chief of staff, frequently held the proxy of the Secretary of War. With few exceptions, Dr. Tugwell usually acted for the Secretary of Agriculture. In the beginning, Solicitor General Biggs often represented the Attorney General and later Judge MacLean, assistant attorney general, took his place. Secretary of Commerce Roper probably has had a higher attendance record than any other Cabinet member of the committee, with the exception of the chairman, and on the rare occasions when he could not be present his place was usually taken by Assistant Secretary Dickinson. Lewis W. Douglas, while serving as Director of the Budget, came only occasionally, but his office was always represented, usually by Charles H. Fullaway, who continued to appear for the Bureau of the Budget after the resignation of Mr. Douglas and the appointment of Daniel W. Bell as acting director. Mr. Battle generally appeared for the Secretary of Labor, while Assistant Secretary of the Treasury Robert was regularly in attendance until Admiral Christian J. Peoples was substituted for him as a member of the Board. Shortly after the appointment of the permanent administrator, Colonel Spalding was recalled to his engineering duties in the army and his place on the Board was taken by Colonel Henry M. Waite, after the latter had been appointed Deputy Administrator. Colonel Sawyer also disappeared from the Board after he ceased to function as Temporary Administrator.

It was quickly decided that the Bureau of Public Roads in the Department of Agriculture, which was experienced in dealing with state-highway boards and in handling road contracts, should be charged with responsibility for expending the road appropriation, subject to the final approval of the Special Board. The details of ship construction were likewise left to the Navy Department.

As subsequent meetings were held, conflicts of opinion developed over many policies. Already it was suggested that the money be spent as quickly as possible without being too meticulous as to graft or value received; while others were urging that the funds be carefully expended only on projects which could be proved to be socially desirable. Then there were geographic questions. Should the money be spent in a limited number of places, or distributed impartially, regardless of where it would do the most good? How should the funds be allotted? How much should go for harbors? How much for housing? How much for Federal projects? How much for municipalities? How much for private enterprises? There also arose the problem of how much interest to charge, and around this was waged a most amazing conflict of opinion —a conflict over the question whether or not we should spend the money at all!

The discussion on this subject arose after a subcommittee appointed to consider the interest rate advised that it was unable to reach an agreement. Dr. Tugwell, chairman of the subcommittee, reported that the majority favored an interest rate of 3½ per cent, but he added that Mr. Douglas, also a member of the subcommittee, did not favor this figure. During the discussion before the entire Board on July 1, the following debate occurred:

Mr. Douglas: Personally, I think the interest rate ought to be 4½ per cent. I feel that apparently the spiral of deflation has come to an end, and the direction of events has turned; that the necessity for injecting an artificial factor into the situation no longer exists to the same extent to which it existed in March or April; that therefore we should put on the brakes, deter municipalities, counties and states from borrowing money, increasing their own indebtedness, and that one of the most effective ways of doing this is by increasing the interest rate.

Dr. Tugwell: Of course Mr. Douglas' suggestion is that we should not spend what is provided for in the bill, and his reason for not doing it is that recovery has already come, or will come if we do not do this. That seems to me to be possible; I do not think it is probable yet, and I do not think that we ought to frame a program based on that assumption.

Mr. Douglas: I do not say that prosperity is here by any manner of means. All I say is that apparently the direction of events has changed and that the necessity which may have existed in March or April, as the facts were then known, to take a great gamble, no longer exists to the same extent.

The Chairman: Of course, this Act, Mr. Director, was passed late in June and the Administration and Congress felt it was necessary to pass some sort of law such as this in order to assure recovery.

Mr. Douglas: Let me ask you this further question: For a depression which has been caused in some measure by excessive debt, how can we hope to pull ourselves out of the depression by increasing the thing that caused it?

The Chairman: Well, that goes to the merits of the Act itself.

Mr. Douglas: Yes, those are pretty fundamental.

The Chairman: But after all, the Act has been passed and we are called upon to administer it.

Mr. Douglas: Yes, that is right; but the Act is entirely permissive, Mr. Secretary, and not mandatory at all. I disagree with Dr. Tugwell on that.

/ . . . . .

Except for Mr. Douglas, the members of the Special Board were not too optimistic about recovery. It was agreed that the public works program should be carried out, as outlined in the Act. The majority of the Board, deciding on a compromise between the 3 per cent preferred by Dr. Tugwell personally, the 3½ per cent recommended by his subcommittee and the 4½ per cent rate advocated by Mr. Douglas, chose 4 per cent, since this charge would not be low enough to attract cities with good financial standing, who could borrow from the usual sources at a lower rate. At the same time, it was felt, in view of the fact that a grant of 30 per cent of the cost of labor and material accompanied most of the loans, this figure would not be so high as to deter borrowers and still assure the Federal Government a fair return on its investment.

Another interesting difference of opinion developed in a discussion of the relative amounts to be appropriated for purely Federal projects as compared with State and municipal projects. It was recognized that Federal projects, because the machinery for getting them under way already existed in the various departments, would start the flow of money more quickly than it could be started by local projects, but it was not certain that they were "socially desirable." The two points of view were brought out at the meeting on June 29, when Secretary Perkins asked how much it had been tentatively decided to allot for Federal projects.

Mr. Robert: About 1 billion 300 million.

Miss Perkins: Is that the soundest kind of economy? It seems to me that it is an extremely bad way to do it. Federal projects do very little to raise the standard of living of the community, do they not?

Mr. Robert: If they are properly applied, I would not agree with you.

Miss Perkins: It is the local projects that raise the standard of living of the communities, and therefore create the wealth out of which later income will flow. In connection with purely Federal public works, they came over and said: "You can get a whole lot of new immigration stations built." All right. We can, if that is desired, and we should treat ourselves to a lot of new immigration stations; but that will not increase or improve the standards of living in the communities in which they are located.

Dr. Tugwell: The Federal projects of the Department of Agriculture are exactly the sort to assist the communities where they are located.

Miss Perkins: Perhaps they are. I do not know anything about those. But certainly immigration detention stations are not going to make any improvement in the local situation. A sewer system would. A sewer system in a certain locality, built out of the locality's own enterprise, would create a situation where the property values of the locality would be improved, and you would have a corresponding increase in the flow of dwellings and industries to that locality, so that you would improve the whole standard of living. The same is true of school buildings. You would get the standard of living improved in that community. But as for improving the standard of living by building immigration detention stations and army posts, it seems to me ridiculous. It does not do anything to improve the standard of living for the people, the taxpayers of the country.

Dr. Tugwell: It does do something to put people back to work.

Miss Perkins: Oh yes, if we are as badly off as that—I mean, if there is no construction to be found in the United States which will raise the standard of living, we will put men to work on building handsome stone walls around private estates. I would be for that, if we had exhausted everything else. If every sewer that needs to be built is built; if every municipal housing project that can reasonably be taken care of is being taken care of; if every bridge that is needed in every community in order to link two important economic units is built; if every grade crossing is eliminated, all of which would improve the standard of living, I would favor other types of projects. But I cannot see the sense of just improving the houses in army posts, or building more houses, or building more immigration detention stations.

Dr. Tugwell: I cannot understand your objection to raising the standard of living in the army. It seems to me it is the same thing.

Miss Perkins: You do not create any wealth by doing that.

Dr. Tugwell: Yes, of course you do.

Miss Perkins: What wealth do you create?

Dr. Tugwell: If you have poor army housing, and it needs to be done over, it seems to me it is just as important as any other housing.

Miss Perkins: If it is just a project to make work, I agree with you. If we have to make work, we will mend the roofs in the army posts, and I think they should be mended, in the ordinary care of property. But to go to work and build new houses, or greatly extend housing facilities, would seem to me to be folly, when there are people in cities who have no houses, or who have rotten, low-grade tenements that need to be rebuilt. If you can build a good tenement housing proposition in a city that needs it, you have created wealth because you have created living quarters where people will go to live and work. You draw population into the area and you create that wealth.

.   .   .   .   .

It was finally decided to keep in mind, so far as possible, the social aspects of projects, so ably expounded by Secretary Perkins, when considering applications for allotments.

A third matter over which divergent points of view developed was the labor policy to be adopted by PWA. It had been apparent from the first that, since the Act provided regulations for wages, hours, local labor and preferences to ex-service men with dependents, it would be necessary to make special findings covering the employment of workers. The choice of men could not be left to

One hundred days, and PWA builds the President a new office.

the contractor, as in private construction, because he would be likely to select those who had worked for him before, regardless of whether they were ex-service men, local residents, or persons desperately in need of work. In many cases the contractor had an employment contract with the union and so would have to accept whatever men the union chose to give him.

To meet this problem, the establishment of employment agencies was agreed upon. Such agencies, the Special Board was advised, had already been authorized by the Wagner-Peyser Act of June 6, 1933, and were in process of being set up under the Department of Labor. To speed their general establishment in the forty-eight States we agreed to finance the entire service (known as the United States Employment Service) which was headed by W. Frank Persons. These agencies should be placed, it was decided, where "selected lists of qualified workers" could be submitted to employers on PWA projects.

Mr. Persons explained to the Board on July 1 that in many cases it would not be necessary to set up a completely new employment service. In States where there already was such a service, he said, it would only be needful to enlarge it.

As soon as the Board's decision was published, the American Federation of Labor informed Secretary Perkins of its fundamental distaste for a government employment service. So violent an objection was made that Miss Perkins reported to the Special Board that the proposal had "created consternation in the hearts of organized labor." The organized groups feared the agencies, with their lists of skilled workers, would supplant union headquarters. To cope with this delicate situation, a Labor Advisory Board was formed by Miss Perkins at the request of the Special Board. Dr. Isador Lubin was selected as chairman and the following labor men were named as members:

John Coefield, president, United Association of Journeymen Plumbers and Steamfitters of the United States and Canada;

Richard J. Gray, treasurer, Bricklayers', Masons' and Plasterers' International Union of America;

George H. Lakey, first vice-president, United Brotherhood of Carpenters and Joiners of America;

Michael J. McDonough, president, Building Trades Department, American Federation of Labor;

Charles L. Read, assistant to the president, International Brotherhood of Electrical Workers of America.

Then organized labor began to make demands upon PWA for special consideration. It became apparent that the organizations were not thinking of the great mass of laboring people who might be benefited by a public works program, but merely of the union worker. We were faced with the problem of working out a solution that would be fair to everybody in accordance with our duty under the law. At first the unions insisted that all workers should be employed through their agencies; we were willing to go so far only as to allow their offices to be used for the hiring of union labor alone. An agreement to this effect carried a proviso that "in the event qualified workers are not furnished by the union locals within forty-eight hours after the request is filed by the employer, such labor may be chosen from lists of qualified workers submitted by local employment agencies designated by the United States Employment Service." All non-union labor was to be obtained from the local agency of the United States Service.

Wages, of course, were a burning question. Labor leaders wanted forty-hour pay for thirty-hour work, but the Board was of the opinion that this was too much. Disregarding the disapproval of union chieftains who opposed a minimum wage on the theory that it usually becomes a maximum wage, we decided to set hourly minimum wages for the country as divided into three zones—Southern, Northern and Central. The scale announced was:

Southern Zone:
      Skilled labor $1.00
      Unskilled labor .... .40

Central Zone:
      Skilled labor 1.10
      Unskilled labor .... .45

Northern Zone:
      Skilled labor 1.20
      Unskilled labor .... .50

The finality of these figures was mitigated by a proviso allowing PWA to accept the union wage rate prevailing in the particular community on April 30, 1933, for the particular type of work involved. This date was determined upon to protect labor against cuts which had taken place in May and August of that year and thus made it possible, under the proviso, for the workers to have the benefit of the 1932 wage scale.

In many cases this meant that workers would get different rates for the same type of employment in the same cities,

depending upon whether they were working on a PWA
project or on a job privately financed. However, we felt
that the policy adopted by PWA was justified since it had
the effect of maintaining labor standards at a reasonable
level. Another cause for a differential in wages in some
localities was the difference in the classification of certain
grades of labor as between skilled and unskilled work.
Whether labor falling in this twilight zone should be paid
the skilled or the unskilled rate was often a confusing
matter to settle and a cause of disputes between union
and non-union forces. To arbitrate all differences resulting from labor troubles, a Board of Labor Review was
established.

Two provisions of the Act itself caused trouble. An
interpretation of the language giving a preference to
veterans was demanded after a United States attorney in
Minnesota had told a union contractor, engaged in building a flying field with union men, many of whom were
not veterans, that he must not hire non-veterans until
every veteran in the locality had been given employment.
A violent union protest resulted.

When the matter was referred to the Attorney General
he gave it as his opinion that Congress had not intended
to disturb the existing conditions of the construction industry by forcing union contractors to give preference to
non-union veterans. He ruled that on union jobs union
veterans should be given preference over other union men,
but denied the right of non-union veterans to precedence
over union non-veterans.

Almost the reverse of this situation arose in a dispute
over the section of the Act giving preference to local labor.

A test of this provision came up in Georgetown, Illinois. This town, with practically no union labor in it, had a heavy relief roll and was granted a PWA loan for a public project. The lowest responsible bidder was a union contractor from the city of Danville in the same county. Preparing to start the work, the contractor said:

"Naturally, as I can't get union labor from Georgetown, I shall have to import it from Danville."

This meant not only that Georgetown would not benefit from this project; it actually would suffer as the result of the increased taxes it would have to pay to liquidate it, while Danville, undergoing no expense, would be able to cut its relief roll and have the advantage resulting from the circulation of money earned by its workmen in a neighboring community. So severe were the objections from Georgetown that fear was expressed lest the angered residents would "blow up the machinery." It was apparent that there would be few applications for non-Federal public works if the labor to be employed was not required to be drawn from the district which was being taxed for the project. Accordingly the contractor was advised to hire the preponderance of his labor from Georgetown even though it was non-union. Union contractors were cautioned that their bids must take into consideration the necessity of using local labor.

One of the most interesting discussions and, from my personal point of view, the most important, revolved around our policy with respect to keeping the program as free as possible from graft, corruption and skimpy work. I think that no one believed for a moment that the huge sum of money at our disposal, or, in fact, any considerable amount of it, could be expended in a vacuum, free from the corrupting influence of the crooked politician, the crooked lobbyist, the crooked contractor and the confirmed grafter. On the plea that Congress intended the money appropriated to be spent as rapidly as possible, it would have been a simple matter to wink at a certain amount of corruption. Perhaps we could have gotten by with credit, or at least without undue criticism, if those connected with PWA had merely refrained from profiting personally or chiseling at the expense of the government. All that would have been required would be to close one's eyes so as not officially to see, and therefore leave one's conscience undisturbed by practices that have been altogether too much taken for granted in this and in other countries in the building of public works. All things considered, should we avail ourselves of every means at our disposal to make sure that the public works program was carried out as honestly and conscientiously as it was humanly possible to do? With this breathtaking sum of taxpayers' money at our disposal, should we make a real attempt to overcome the cynical belief that no governmental body can be trusted with a large sum of money?

Many persons, some of them honest and sincere at that, were clearly of the opinion that the public works program ought to go ahead with speed as its object; that we should adopt the conventional attitude toward a project after the contract had been let on competitive bids; that we should take steps to protect ourselves from any major scandal, but that we were simply too busy helping bring about recovery to pay any attention to the ordinary graft and waste that have come to be taken for granted in the building of public works. If it was a question of speed with some graft versus a slower program without graft, those entertaining the point of view just described preferred speed.

At the first meeting of the Special Board, this whole issue was brought out by Secretary Roper and placed squarely before us so that no one could avoid seeing it. It is interesting to quote from Secretary Roper's statements on that occasion:

"The men around this table are charged with a weighty responsibility to the American people, to this Administration. It is going to be watched; all kinds of charges are going to be preferred, referring to every kind of detail. I would like to know at this juncture, in connection with the point that I am going to raise, whether you contemplate having a research group—a group of people who will go away beyond what we contemplate doing this afternoon and will be studying with this in view. I am touching upon a question of policy. We must look into the future, for a program that looks toward a more permanent situation than we are now contemplating. What are we looking forward to as a permanent highway for the American people? If you will let that be known then you will give to the taxpayers of this country a hope of relief.

"Now the question of graft is constantly coming up. Just anticipate it. Every man who allocates money should be bonded and it should be told to the American people. We are working out an arrangement here by which the taxpayers of this country, this Administration, this government, are going to be protected at every juncture.

"And then I think of the question of preferential treatment. What I refer to is the fellow that ordinarily is called a lobbyist; we ought to send him where he belongs; don't let the fellow who wants a contract think he can send someone down to Washington who is a Democrat, who has all influence here, and who can take somebody out to lunch and fix him. I am constantly asked by people wiring me, 'Can't you lunch with me?' I am now set off from even lunching with my friends. What I am after is, if there ever was a time in the history of this country when we have got to be like Cæsar's wife, it is now; and the best thing we can do to give this thing a send-off is to plan very carefully your first impression on the people. Therefore, with this whole question of policy in mind, Mr. Chairman, I believe it would be worth your while, as it would expedite consideration, for you to appoint a small committee associated with the Administration, including ourselves, who will apply themselves for the next day or two to that question of policy."

Ever since I became interested in public affairs, I have contested vigorously the generally accepted theory of the cynics that it is useless to expect the government service to be either particularly honest or efficient. I admit there has been altogether too much corruption and inefficiency in our various governments. Some of our municipalities have been run in a scandalous fashion. Many county governments have been wasteful and inefficient or worse, and at times even certain of our State administrations have not been free from suspicion. There also have been occasions when crooks and grafters have had tainted connections with the Federal Government. Just in passing it might be asked who is responsible for corruption in government when it exists? Those who do the corrupting are the seekers after favors from government, either in the way of special privileges or of unconscionable profits on materials sold to government or contracts performed for government. On the charge of corruption government officials do not stand as the only prisoners in the dock awaiting trial in the court of public opinion.

Without attempting to discount the great need for speed, the Special Board took the position that there were other considerations which it was its duty to regard. It considered the establishment of a reputation for honesty and efficiency on the part of the Federal Government to be a very important thing of itself. We decided to go ahead as quickly as possible, at the same time, however, demanding the safeguards that we would have insisted upon if the money had been our own to spend in our own private interest. We set before ourselves at the outset the perhaps unattainable ideal of administering the greatest fund for construction in the history of the world without scandal that was preventable.

We also had to determine at once whether or not to give money to the various departments and bureaus of the Federal Government to augment their greatly reduced budgets. As soon as the Act was passed and it was understood that the money was to be spent to put men to work, a flood of requests for funds came from the departments. It was argued that the money could be used for socially desirable and extremely necessary work, and it was pointed out that they had been so badly curtailed by the Douglas budget that many of the bureaus were actually in danger of having to discontinue essential activities. The departments and agencies were voted money in cases where they could show that it would be spent to put men to work on socially desirable projects, and the Special Board also financed the operations of various emergency organizations that were parts of the recovery set-up. Ultimately the statutory, executive and special allotments for purposes other than construction, but including allocations for roads, naval vessels, CWA, CCC, etc., amounted to more than 1 billion 12 million dollars.

This set a definite, and not generally known, limitation on the money that could be spent directly for construction by PWA. Many refer roundly to the sum of 3 billion 300 million dollars as having been expended by PWA for public works. The figure is actually only 2 billion 730 millions, including 50 millions for the Tennessee Valley Authority and a little more than 8 millions for relief highways. However, the total appropriations handled by the Board up to April 1, 1935, amount to $3,757,-670,833 of which 3 billion 300 million came under the original Act, 400 millions more by virtue of the Emergency Appropriation Act of 1934, and $57,670,833 from the sale of bonds to the RFC as of the date of April 1, 1935.* The sale of the bonds so far has netted a gain of more than a million dollars over the value for which the bonds were accepted by PWA.

Drawn up hastily and passed in a breath by the Congress, the Act apparently contradicted itself with respect to

---

* Later 310 millions were impounded by the President out of unappropriated and unobligated balances in order to finance the Federal Emergency Relief Administration pending passage of the Emergency Relief Appropriation Act of 1935. This money was not returned to PWA.

the policies to be adopted in making loans to States and municipalities. Legal interpretations were necessary. In Title II of the Act it is clearly stated that PWA must obtain reasonable security for such loans. But in section 203-D the Act says:

"The President, in his discretion, and under such terms as he may prescribe, may extend any of the benefits of this title to any State, county or municipality notwithstanding any constitutional or legal restriction or limitation on the right or power of such State, county or municipality to borrow money or incur indebtedness."

Obviously, the point of conflict that arose was as to whether or not PWA had the right to extend loans to municipaliies and States which had already reached the limits of their constitutional powers to incur debts. It is impossible to exact "reasonable security" from governments which are already beyond the limits imposed by State constitutions or municipal charters.

What to do about this apparent conflict in the Act itself gave rise to a debate among the members of the Board on July 6. Mr. Robert insisted that Senator Russell of Georgia had put clause 203-D in the Act because nearly thirty States, including his own, as the result of constitutional debt limitations, would be unable to secure loans without constitutional amendments which it might take two or three years to effect. In some cases even this remedy would be of no avail.

When Secretary Dern asked if the clause meant that the President could give such States what in law would amount to a gift, it was pointed out that this would discriminate unfairly against States that could not get money except on a loan and grant basis backed by good security. The Board debated the matter at length:

Mr. Robert: In his good judgment he (the President) can grant anything he wants to.

Mr. Dickinson: There is this difficulty about it. If the Act only gives him authority to loan money, he cannot go ahead and loan it if these people cannot borrow any money. They cannot give him any obligation for the money, so it would not be a loan.

Mr. Robert: It does not define what loaning and borrowing are in this case. The purpose of the Act is to relieve unemployment, and that is why the machinery is set up. The President can grant a loan, and defer an election for two or three years at his discretion.

Dr. Tugwell: Are you going to use this to defeat the two provisions in the law which say that they must have balanced budgets?

Mr. Robert: The President will be the judge of that. That is exactly the come-back he has. "Gentlemen," he will be able to say, "you come here and want 10 million dollars. Show me that your house is in order." "We have borrowed all we can borrow," they will reply, "but our house is in order." "Very well, we will let you have this 10 million dollars and arrange the terms later. Go to work on the project." If he can't do that, we will be here two or three years trying to decide who is going to get the money.

Mr. Biggs: How are you going to collect it?

Mr. Robert: It has always been my theory that the government could collect any time it wants to, if it has the proper machinery.

Mr. Biggs: Suppose the State of Georgia wanted 25 million dollars and they had borrowed up to the limit and the President let them have 25 million dollars. How is he going to get it back?

Mr. Robert: I have been lending money all my life and have never been able to get it back. I am weak in that respect.

Mr. Dern: But no valid obligation could be given.

Mr. Biggs: If the President begins to lend money to communities that cannot make a valid note or bond, we will be in a terrible fix.

Mr. Robert: We are trying to define between actually giving away 500 million dollars in emergency relief, on the one hand, and, on the other hand, trying to find a reasonable excuse to say that we are lending it to the community. We are not looking for an ironbound, RFC self-liquidating loan by any means. If we were we might just as well quit operating now and just devote ourselves to Federal projects and let these others alone. We ought to be in the position of looking for a means, rather than making the other fellow come to us, except to the extent of keeping his house in order. It seems to me it is the one opportunity for the President to say, "If you get your machinery down to where it is economical we will do business with you." It is just like a bank. When you go to a bank the banker will finance you if he knows that you have cut your overhead and done certain things. This is the same sort of a proposition.

Mr. Biggs: He will not do business with you unless you can give a valid obligation.

Mr. Robert: The bank might be in with you so deeply

—as the government is in this case—in your little manufacturing plant, that it would be anxious to go along with you so that you could survive. That is the position the government is in with its people to-day. We are anxious to keep them going until we have a recovery.

Colonel Sawyer: I have talked with hundreds of people and have had hundreds of letters on this subject. My observation is that in the great majority of cases we can work our way out of this quickly and at the same time have a legal contract. I think, to satisfy good business practice, we will have to have that, and I do not think it will slow things up. In some cases it will mean an election, which may take two or three or four weeks. Meantime there is a lot of perfecting of the plans and specifications to be done; so I do not think it is going to sacrifice any time. But I think we must approach it from the purely legal standpoint.

Mr. Dern: We can do some of these things, if necessary, by organizing private corporations.

Colonel Sawyer: The "authority" idea appeals to me.

Mr. Robert: I do not know about the private corporation idea, but you will find in many of these communities, gentlemen, that a bond issue will not pass. They will be more interested in knowing that the graft is cut out of local government, and that is the one hammer the President has in this instance. That is one place where I agree 100 per cent with Director Douglas. Now is the time to see that money is available to the ones in shape to take it. I know in my own town of Atlanta the city would rise up and cheer if this law were laid down there, and they would not vote for any amount of bonds unless they knew that was the case. That is the reason they will not vote. You could call an election to-morrow and it would not pass.

I am a little off the subject, but I feel that this is the spirit of this Act, and we ought to get the best possible legal paper. We are giving away 500 million dollars for emergency relief, and we trying to get as close to our legal paper as possible.

Mr. Dern: I can say I have a great deal of sympathy with your viewpoint, Mr. Robert, but it seems to be somewhat in conflict with some of the things we have already adopted here at former meetings. We have been rather insistent upon all these things being in the shape of loans, and that there shall be amortization, and a fixed rate of interest.

.   .   .   .   .

An investigation of the legal possibilities of finding a way to make loans to States restricted by their constitutions was left to the staff of the newly appointed chief attorney, Mr. Hunt, but the general policy of not making loans without security was decided by the Board.

Another matter which had to be settled before men could be put to work was the general set-up of PWA. Plans had been made under General Johnson to give broad authority to the State engineer which would permit him to pass upon public works projects within his jurisdiction and see that they were properly carried out. The engineer was to be practically the final authority, although responsible in a rather indefinite way to the Administrator in Washington. Obviously, forty-eight independent engineers acting on their own uncontrolled authority could authorize about forty-eight times as many projects in the same space of time as a single engineer in Washington.

But the Special Board, intent upon making sure that the money would be spent on the proper kind of projects, saw many difficulties in connection with a decentralized organization so loosely put together as in effect to be without responsibility to anyone. It would be an impossibility to check upon the activities of forty-eight engineers unless they could be made strictly accountable to the Administrator in Washington. Moreover, there was not available the trained personnel necessary to set up forty-eight complete State organizations.

It was accordingly decided that each State should have an engineer-administrator with an advisory board of three, the States to be grouped into ten regions in charge of each of which there would be a regional adviser. These latter were to act as field marshals, while the Washington headquarters staff would have appellate jurisdiction to study all projects from their legal, engineering and financial aspects. The State boards, acting with the State engineers, could recommend that a project be accepted or rejected but Washington reserved the final decision.

Later it became necessary to subdivide the work at Washington into appropriate divisions. A housing division, for instance, was set up to have primary jurisdiction over low-cost housing and slum-clearance projects, with Robert D. Kohn in charge. A transportation division to pass upon applications from railroads for loans, was likewise established under Frank C. Wright. Later, when electric power development came in for special consideration, an Electric Power Board of Review was created to co-ordinate and expedite the examination of projects within this field.

The division of projects into Federal and non-Federal was purely accidental. Colonel Sawyer, as Temporary Administrator, had received a number of requests for public works funds from various governmental departments and bureaus. He kept these in a "Federal" category. Then, from the Reconstruction Finance Corporation, came a separate list of applications for "non-Federal" self-liquidating loans. This natural classification of projects as Federal and non-Federal has persisted.

The discussions over labor, the interest rate on loans, the advisability of going ahead at all with the program, to what extent we should insist upon honesty and efficiency, are examples of problems raised at every Board meeting. Others were equally important but there is no point in citing more than enough to give an idea of the type of questions that we were called upon to grapple with. As pointed out in the preceding chapter, we were in virgin territory, faced with the necessity of blazing our own trails through the mountains and the valleys of policy, of cutting through the legal underbrush to our goal. Moreover, we had to reach that goal—the complete allocation of the 3 billion 300 million dollars—as quickly as possible, yet without waste or graft.

Somehow we managed to keep going through all the enervating month of that first July, drawing up tentative policies, accepting some and rejecting others; arguing, discussing and pondering. We started early and worked late each day and finally, on July 31, we issued Circular

No. 1 of the Federal Emergency Board of Public Works containing an outline of the purposes, policies, functions and organization of PWA. This circular enumerated the tests to be applied to public works projects as follows:

1. The relation of the particular project to coördinated planning, and its social desirability.

2. Its economic desirability; that is, its relation to unemployment and the revival of industry.

3. The soundness of the project from an engineering and technical standpoint.

4. The financial ability of the applicant to complete the work and reasonably to secure any loans made by the United States.

5. The legal collectibility of the securities to be purchased by the United States or the enforceability of any lease to be entered into between the applicant and the United States.

The following labor policies were listed:

1. Opportunities for employment shall be equitably distributed among the qualified workers who are unemployed, not among those who merely wish to change one good job for another.

2. Opportunities shall be distributed geographically as widely and as equitably as possible.

3. Qualified workers who, under the law are entitled to preference, shall be given such preference.

4. The wastefulness and personal disappointments resulting from unwarranted migration of labor in quest of work shall be avoided.

5. Local labor shall, so far as practicable, be selected from lists of qualified workers submitted by local employment agencies designated by the United States Employment Service. Highly skilled or organized labor shall not be required to register for work at such agencies, but may be secured in the customary way through recognized trade union locals.

6. No convict labor shall be employed.

7. So far as practicable, no individual directly employed shall be permitted to work more than thirty hours in any one week, and all employees shall be paid just and reasonable wages sufficient to provide a decent and comfortable standard of living.

Chapter III

ORGANIZING FOR THE JOB

It did not take me long, after the President had set up the Public Works Board by executive order, to realize that we had a machine that could not function. Immediately upon signing the order, the President had left Washington for a cruise north along the Atlantic Coast. He badly needed a vacation and none of us begrudged it to him. From the moment he was sworn in as President, he had had thrust upon his shoulders the heaviest burdens that any President in our history has been called upon to assume in the same length of time. He had been working day and night, grappling with problems of tremendous import to the American people. He had outlined a program for economic and social rehabilitation and the Congress had implemented it. It had in effect said to him, "We freely give you the most extraordinary powers ever conferred upon a President of the United States in full confidence that you can and will use them for the benefit of the sorely pressed American people."

Subordinates of the Administration cheerfully agreed to carry on to the best of their ability during the absence of the President. So far as PWA was concerned, the responsibility imposed upon us was a heavy one. Three billions three hundred millions of dollars had been appropriated by the Congress with which to undertake and carry through a public works program. It was our duty not only to provide work on worth-while and socially desirable public works projects; it was our especial duty to provide work as quickly as possible in the hope that the calling of men back to work at fair wages would have the effect of setting in motion the mired wheels of commerce and industry.

To undertake this gigantic task we had no machinery at hand and no precedent to guide us. The seas were uncharted. If there was any works plan in existence anywhere, we were not informed of it. We had to find projects upon which we could expend public funds within the limitations imposed by Congress, and we had to develop an administrative technique that could effectuate the object that we had in view.

Colonel Sawyer had been appointed Temporary Administrator. Soon it became apparent that it would be necessary, if our program was to go ahead as it was intended that it should, to appoint an Administrator who was, above all things else, an executive who could drive ahead regardless of all obstacles. If the President should ask me to suggest a man for Administrator or Deputy Administrator, I wanted to be in a position to give him the name of a first-rate man. My mind began to cast about for an engineer, but I had had practically no contact with engineers. Accordingly, I telephoned to my old friend, Professor Charles E. Merriam, chairman of the Department of Political Science at the University of Chicago, asking him if he could suggest an engineer of ability, experience and unquestioned character, who could be given a place of high command in the Public Works Administration. I did this without consulting any of my colleagues and merely for the purpose of informing myself. Professor Merriam, as I learned later, consulted Louis Brownlow who recommended Colonel Henry M. Waite of Cincinnati, Ohio.

I did not know Colonel Waite, but I looked him up at once and found his background and experience to be fine in every particular. The grandson of a former Chief Justice of the United States, he had had a rich and varied career. Moreover, to my surprise, I found that he was in Washington, having been called here to assist in building up the anticipatory public works organization that had been initiated by General Hugh S. Johnson. I sent for Colonel Waite and that first interview left me with a high regard for him that has never abated since. I told him that it was clear to me that we would have to have an immediate reorganization of public works upon the President's return and that I wanted to be able to suggest him as a possibility for a place high in that organization, if he was in a position to serve. He said that he had come to Washington for that purpose and would be glad to have a part in the program.

PWA continued to mark time. There was a lack of driving leadership; there was no energy in its functioning. We had a Board, of which I was the chairman, but a board never can perform as an executive. It always has been my firm conviction that no executive job of any size can be handled competently by a board. A great organization can never be built up, nor can it operate efficiently even after it has been built up, if a debating society is substituted for the effective, single executive at the top that such

a situation imperatively demands. As chairman of the
Board, I did not consider that I had authority really to
take hold of the Public Works Administration and run it
even if I had the necessary qualities for such a job. I sus-
pect that Colonel Sawyer felt that he was under a handicap because he had been named merely as Temporary
Administrator. There was an implication in the situation
that it was the purpose of the President not to continue
the temporary set-up of PWA beyond the period of his
vacation.

The President had asked those members of the Cabinet
who would be in Washington to meet him aboard the
U.S.S. *Indianapolis* at Annapolis on July 4, 1933. Several
of us did meet him and among other matters discussed
informally were the public works organization and program. I told him frankly that in my judgment a reorganization was needed at once if we were to go ahead
seriously with the program. Secretary Roper, who was
also a member of the Public Works Board and with whom
I had discussed the situation, expressed the same opinion.
The President indicated that he had already come to that
conclusion, apparently on the basis of facts that had
reached him from independent sources. No names were
suggested and none was asked for, but it was known that
there were one or two men expectantly sitting under that
particular plum tree with their mouths open hoping for
the best.

The following week-end I was in Chicago where I had
gone to deliver the commencement address at Lake Forest
College. Returning to Washington the morning of July 8,
1933, I was told at my office that the President wanted to

see me as soon as possible. I called Colonel McIntyre, who made an appointment for me with the President. In the latter's office, also waiting for him when I went over for my interview, was Assistant Secretary Robert. He held his hand out saying that he wanted to congratulate me. I asked him what for and he said, "The President is going to make you Public Works Administrator." I remarked that that was surprising news to me. I had not been a candidate for the position and had never for a moment harbored the thought that the President was considering me. Mr. Robert assured me that the thing was all settled and that the executive order appointing me had been already prepared.

Shortly thereafter the President came in and, after his manner, without preliminaries, he officially confirmed the information that I had already received. He did not ask me whether I wanted to be Public Works Administrator; he simply told me that he was naming me Public Works Administrator. Naturally, I accepted the assignment. I left the White House for my office in the Interior Building in somewhat of a daze—entrusted with a responsibility probably greater than had ever been given an officer of the government, other than the President, in time of peace, since the country was founded. I was elated, of course, at the confidence that the President had shown in me, but this feeling hardly weighed in the scales as against the sense of responsibility that I felt. I did not need to be told that the manner in which this huge fund was to be administered might make or break the Administration.

My first official act as Administrator of public works

Welding joints in the reinforcing steel used in the concrete pipe for the water supply line from the Hetch-Hetchy dam in the Yosemite Valley. Besides providing an adequate water supply system for the next sixty or seventy-five years, this PWA project will provide 26,700 man-months of direct employment.

was to send for Colonel Waite and tell him that he was Deputy Administrator. From that point on PWA really began to function.

While this was the effective beginning of the final administrative set-up for PWA it was by no means the first attempt to create such an organization. Quite the reverse. As a matter of fact there had already been four plans for the administrative staff and two working organizations.

Before the President had signed his executive order creating the Board of Public Works with Colonel Sawyer as Temporary Administrator, Colonels Spalding and Waite and their staff had been busy putting the finishing touches on an organization that had been started even before the National Industrial Recovery Act had received the President's signature. They had prepared charts of projects and compiled lists of names available for State engineers. Busy as they were in staffing a hypothetical organization, they later found themselves outdone by Colonel Sawyer who, with his staff of seventeen men from the Federal Emergency Stabilization Board, was also hard at work listing projects and filling in the names of prospective personnel on organization charts.

Still other plans of organization were in the making by the members of the self-liquidating division of the Reconstruction Finance Corporation which was about to be disbanded because all of its projects were in course of being transferred to PWA. Finally a fourth set of charts was being drawn, under the direction of Assistant Secretary Robert of the Treasury Department, which had always been in charge of the construction of public buildings.

At the time he had created the Public Works Board the President instructed me to move the PWA staff into the Interior Building so that there should be a distinct line of demarcation between PWA and the NRA code administrations which were under the authority of General Johnson. Room had been squeezed out of the Interior Building for Colonel Sawyer and the few members who then constituted his staff. Then the Spalding-Waite staff conceived the notion of moving into the same building and Major Crawford and Colonel Clark were directed to find the necessary office space. The Spalding-Waite personnel, which for the most part had been rendering volunteer service, was placed on the payroll and paid from the date of the passage of the National Industrial Recovery Act to June 24, 1933, on which date they were separated from the service. Most of them were immediately reëmployed and brought into the Interior Building, among the number being Colonel Waite and Henry T. Hunt. As chief counsel, Mr. Hunt immediately began the task of drafting PWA Circular No. 1.

Probably no member of that original PWA organization ever comprehended the magnitude of the fortune entrusted to it. It is fair to say that not one of them was able to visualize how much money 3 billion 300 million dollars really was. Few people can even encompass such a sum within their imaginations. It helped me to estimate its size by figuring that if we had it all in currency and should load it into trucks we could set out with it from Washington for the Pacific Coast, shovel off one million dollars at every milepost and still have enough left to build a fleet of battleships. That's how much money 3 billion 300 mil-

lion dollars is. That was the sum that the President had
entrusted to us. It was up to the Public Works Administration to write whatever record, for good or for ill, was
to be made.

It is not to be wondered at that the first deep concern
of the Administrator was to bring order into the organization. He has always congratulated himself that
he made a fine start when he selected Colonel Waite as
Deputy Administrator, but in order to spend this great sum
of money in the interest of the people, whose money it
was, it was necessary to set up an efficient and trustworthy
machine. He had to iron out the kinks resulting from a
multiplicity of organization plans and from the clashing
of personal ambitions that had led to the setting up of the
nuclei of four different staffs. This difficult problem was surrounded by a palisade of question marks.
How big an organization would be needed? Guesses ran
all the way from one engineer and one lawyer to a staff
of five thousand persons. What type of organization
would be most efficient? Could it be built around the
framework of any existing group? Should it have the
three main divisions of the temporary Spalding-Waite
organization—engineering, legal and finance?

Complicating these problems was the pressing necessity for speed. We soon realized that we would
require many engineers, lawyers, financial experts and
accountants, to say nothing of a host of lesser executives,
as well as stenographers and clerks. Man power had to
be assembled quickly. The whole country was searched
for the right kind of personnel. It was possible to pick
up a few employees that the economy program of the

Administration had loosed from other departments, but these were only a handful. We had to get a staff right away because everyone was looking to Washington for precious work, and work had to be created by means of Federal, State and municipal projects of an enduring quality that would give direct employment to carpenters, bricklayers and road builders, and indirect employment to men in factories and machine shops and on the railroads who would be called upon to fabricate and transport the materials that were to be builded into the public works.

The formation and staffing of what in short order became a great organization to carry out the mandate of Congress and the wishes of the President was completed almost over night. Yet the record of this achievement is one of which every member of PWA is proud. Himself one of the great engineers of the country, Colonel Waite proceeded to surround himself with engineers who had done great things. There were brought from the four corners of America men who had built bridges and dams and monumental buildings. When in August of 1934 Colonel Waite resigned to pioneer a new field of reëmployment economics in Cincinnati his work was ably taken over by Major Philip B. Fleming, who had been his right-hand man from the beginning.

It was equally important to have a staff of keen lawyers. We already had Henry T. Hunt, and from the Reconstruction Finance Corporation came Edward H. Foley, Jr., a man young in years but mature in thought and ripe in judgment, who shortly became the administrative head of the legal staff, while Mr. Hunt as chief counsel devoted himself to exploring intricate legal questions that required special attention. Lloyd H. Landau gave up a highly remunerative practice in St. Louis for the love of the public service and for the opportunity to be close to the late Justice Oliver Wendell Holmes, whose legal secretary he had been at one time. Benjamin V. Cohen, protégé of that fine citizen and jurist, Judge Julian W. Mack, of the United States Circuit Court of Appeals, came from New York to endear himself to the whole staff with his gentle ways and his brilliant mind. Other lawyers from east, from west, from north and from south, were gathered together until we had well over one hundred working in the Washington offices alone.

As it was part of our plan to lend money for non-Federal projects which would require the pledging of State, municipal and other bonds as security, we needed the services of a man able and experienced in public bonds. To give us a leg up, the Prudential Insurance Company patriotically loaned us the services of Lewis B. Mansfield for three months. Under his able guidance we gathered together a group of men who knew all the intricacies of bonds. The competent organization thus thrown together, after Mr. Mansfield had gone back to his company, was placed under the charge of Philip M. Benton. To our lasting satisfaction, Frank C. Wright, vice-president of the Bangor and Aroostook Railroad, was persuaded to handle our railroad loans. Clarence McDonough was appointed director of the engineering division.

Realizing that the people would be interested in knowing what this young Goliath was doing to help in the recovery movement and that they were entitled to be informed, in the early days of PWA Michael W. Straus, one of the star correspondents of the International News Service, was drafted to head up the public relations division. To Louis R. Glavis, the man who had been discharged from the service of the government for uncovering the Ballinger scandals during the Taft administration, but to whom President Roosevelt had restored his civil service status, and who had been made director of investigations of the Department of the Interior, was entrusted the duty of protecting the vast system of public works from the grafter, the exploiter, the chiseler, the cheating contractor, and the crooked politician. Under Howard A. Gray there was organized an inspection division composed of engineers whose duty it was to make sure that every public works project was built strictly according to the specifications. Personnel matters were placed in the capable hands of E. K. Burlew, a career man, who was also handling administrative matters in the Department of the Interior in addition to being budget officer of that department. After our staff had all been set up and we had time to count noses, we found that in Washington alone we had a total of more than 2,300 persons.

After we had gotten fairly under way in building up our central organization we set about the establishment of abbreviated organizations throughout the country. We divided the Nation into ten arbitrary regions and over each region appointed a regional director. In each State we set up a group consisting of a State engineer and a State advisory board, the latter composed of three persons. These boards were strictly non-partisan. Appointments were made on the basis of ability and character, and by the express orders of the President, Republicans as well as Democrats were chosen. Each of these State organizations had a staff sufficient for its needs. When the PWA organization was at its maximum of man power, there was employed in its service throughout the country a total of 3,735 persons.

It was a notable achievement, this gathering together of a staff of expert and trained men and women to undertake this huge new task for the people of the United States. But the physical accomplishment was, after all, not nearly so noteworthy as the fact that this large group, few of whom had known each other before, most of whom were strangers to Washington, and all of whom had no conception of the magnitude of the task they were called upon to undertake, came together and, practically without disorder and with a minimum of friction, clicked into a well-coördinated, smoothly functioning machine that has continued ever since to work efficiently and with great esprit de corps for the United States Government. It may also be pridefully recorded that the dismissals for cause from this organization have been negligible and that resignations for other than weighty personal reasons have been almost non-existent.

But even before we had begun to collect our staff, we went to work on the allocation of loans for public works projects. We were determined that some of the money should move at once, and I asked Colonel Waite to prepare a list of RFC projects which we could take over. The resultant search through the RFC records was swift and exhaustive. Lights blazed in the Interior Building throughout most of the ensuing nights; groups of engi-

neers and lawyers pored over the mass of documents relating to each of the hundreds of applications made to
the RFC by municipalities all over the country, sifting,
sorting, rejecting, approving. The building had some of
the tense atmosphere of a general staff headquarters after
a declaration of war. Indeed, we had declared war on
depression!

The engineers and lawyers, out of the pile, quickly
selected twenty-four applications for municipal water-
works and sewer systems, scaling from $100,000 down to
$6,000. These projects, totaling slightly less than one
million dollars, were approved by the President on July
13, "subject to the execution of a contract between the
applicant and the United States, satisfactory to the
Administrator."

This was only the beginning of a period of tremendously
hard work which lasted for months. As the flood of new
applications came in from Florida to Oregon, from California to Maine, it almost became the rule for the staff
to work at night, and even on Saturday afternoons and
Sundays, without extra compensation.

At the same time the staff was growing. The small
salaries that we could offer handicapped us in our choice
of men, but we got around this difficulty by picking, particularly in the case of lawyers, intelligent and highly
trained younger men willing to work for the wages we
could pay. They were chosen on the basis of fitness and
character from junior partners in well-established law
firms or from honor men recently graduated from the leading law schools. The result was a legal staff of ability
well above the average. Another handicap was the lack

of space in the Interior Building. We considered it necessary to keep the PWA staff together under one roof and
men had to be herded into small offices to do this. Eventually we became so crowded that we were forced to move
out some of the regular Interior Department bureaus in
order to make room.

Still another difficulty was occasioned by the political
pressure brought to bear on us for administrative jobs. It
seemed, at times, as though everybody in the country,
both male and female, had worked for years for the
Democratic Party at great personal sacrifice and that
every one of these persons had fixed upon a berth with
PWA as his reward. Certain political leaders sent literally
thousands of job-seekers to us. I had a sympathetic understanding of the pressure brought to bear by constituents
upon their Congressmen. I wanted to give every possible
aid to them in their patronage difficulties but I made up
my mind never to sacrifice the efficiency of the organization to politics. After all the best politics for PWA was
an absence of politics.

The same policy of putting efficiency above political
expediency was carried out in the actual administering of
the money as well as in the selection of the personnel of
the machine which was to administer PWA. These questions were asked from the first: Are powerful local politicians to be allowed to build palatial postoffices in dying
crossroad villages? Are incompetents to be employed
merely because they have strong political backing? Are
contracts to be shot through with graft and profiteering?
In short, is PWA to be another pork barrel?

The answer to these and similar questions was that if

the President had intended to use this money for partisan or political purposes he would have asked Congress to apportion it in the Public Works Bill according to the old log-rolling system. He would not have appointed any Republicans on the regional and State advisory boards. He would not have told me that he wanted a non-political administration. Nor would he have approved the safeguards which we proceeded to develop in order to minimize waste, graft and political influence.

When I became Administrator a deluge of pleas for funds had already descended upon us, and had we acted without investigation on all the suggestions and requests we would have been able to allot every cent of our appropriation within a month. The pressure from local communities was tremendous. Delegations of politicians, business men, contractors and "leading citizens" laid siege to our offices in person, by mail, by telephone and by telegraph. Among the pleas for special favor that inundated us the most insistent and insidious were attempts of private business to snuggle under the wing of public works on the pretext that the project advocated was municipal.

A delegation comes in with the usual pomp and circumstance and says:

"We represent the city of So-and-so. We want to build a tobacco (or cheese, or lumber or candy) factory. It will give work to our unemployed and will be a fine thing for the city."

"Does the city itself intend to operate this factory?" we ask.

There is a long pause.

"No," finally says the leader of the delegation. "The

city intends to lease it out to some experts qualified in that business."

Of course, we had no authority to lend for such a purpose. And if we made a check, we usually found that the "qualified experts" were promoters with political influence who wanted to start a business of their own. Unable to obtain loans through the regular banking channels, they conceived the clever idea of approaching Uncle Sam as a beneficent old relative who might give them Federal money to hazard in a new enterprise.

In one large city the aldermen sat down one afternoon to decide what their city needed from the public works fund. Each statesman put forward his pet project. When they added up the total they found that they needed 420 million dollars right away.

A persistent correspondent urged us to commission 10,000 men, at $1,000 a year each, to eliminate corporeal snakes from the United States. The cost of these modern St. Patricks would have been a modest $10,000,000 a year.

One project, hailed by its proponents as strictly self-liquidating, was for a maternity hospital in a medium-sized city. Investigation disclosed that it could be paid for if every woman in town would have a baby each year for the following twenty years.

A request for funds to build a graveyard was turned down when it was discovered that the loan, to be liquidated, would entail the death of everyone in the community within 17 years.

Probably the most original idea, however, came from a mathematician who suggested that we set aside 100 million dollars to finance a round-trip passenger-carrying rocket to the moon. With all deference to the professor, the likelihood of making this a paying proposition was too problematical to be considered. Moreover, our program was national, not interplanetary.

But it was with respect to funds for the various States, as well as in apportioning new public buildings among clamant localities, that the greatest pressure was exerted.

As I have shown, the idea back of this Act, new in our national policy, was that Congress should appropriate a lump sum and turn it over to the President, who, through a Public Works Administrator, might spend it according to a national need and a national plan, without regard to politics.

The change is a revolutionary one. It is in line with what students of government have been urging for years. Whether we shall stick to our new policy in the future, or revert to the pork barrel, may depend, in large measure, upon how honestly, impartially and ably the present funds are administered.

Yet this new and concededly better policy cannot of itself change human nature. The appetite for pork, pampered for a century, cannot be legislated out of existence by an act of Congress. A drug addict is not able to return to normal health by virtue of a New Year's resolution.

Representatives and senators, governors and mayors, have not been idle. In all fairness it should be recognized that their position is a difficult one. The people back home say, "You're a big man. We elected you. Here's 3 billion 300 million dollars to be spent. You mean to say you can't get a cent of it for us?" And what has made it especially hard is that every locality has had its own desperate problem of human need and unemployment on its hands. Yet if we had started to yield in individual cases, the whole principle would have been lost, waste would have crept in and national planning would have been forgotten. Accordingly we have tried with all our hearts to consider every local problem presented from the point of view of what would be best for the country as a whole.

To explain the machinery that was developed to cope with the emergency, let us take an imaginary project through the mill. Naturally we cannot find one that will contain every problem, but we can, at least, show in general our processes and the safeguards we have set up.

Suppose the city of Jonesville, somewhere in the Middle West, has a sewage system which is old and inadequate, and which is polluting both the river which runs along the outskirts and the beaches of the nearby lake. For a long time everyone has agreed that the town should have a new system but, because of falling taxes and bad times, Jonesville hasn't had the money to go ahead. The city council did go far enough to hire a good engineer to make an estimate of the cost of a new sewage system, but when he reported that it would cost $500,000 to build, the plans were reluctantly shelved.

Then the Public Works Act is passed. Nearby towns are getting allocations for municipal projects. A State engineer of PWA comes into the city and calls on the mayor.

"Why haven't you got some business for us?" he asks. "You don't mean to say your city is perfect?"

"Far from it," the mayor replies sadly, "but where are we going to get half a million dollars for a new sewage system?"

"You can get $150,000 from the PWA as an outright grant and we will lend you the rest."

The mayor asks, "How can we borrow any more money? We've already issued bonds up to our legal limit and our municipal finances are in a pretty bad way."

"You still have a good chance to borrow money from the PWA. If legally you can lay a service tax on the new sewage system, say by charging the user so much for every tap, toilet and bathtub, so that the revenue produced will pay off the loan in not to exceed 30 years at 4 per cent interest, then you can get the money, both $150,000 grant and $350,000 loan. Otherwise, under the law, we have no power to let you have it."

After several such talks, the mayor becomes enthusiastic. With the approval of the city council, he makes an application to the State Advisory Board for a grant and loan. The State engineer for PWA and the board look the project over, find that it is worthy and practicable, and hurry it on to Washington.

In Washington the Jonesville sewage application is taken by the project division and copies of it are sent to each of the three examining divisions—engineering, finance and legal. This concurrent examination saves a great deal of time.

The copy sent to the engineering division is given to an engineer whose specialty is sewage systems. He examines the plans, looks up the geographical situation of Jonesville, breaks down the request for $500,000 into the items allowed for labor, material, the purchase of land, interest, and other expenses, and then goes over the whole project with meticulous care. Particularly he asks if the allowance for labor and material is in accord with prices prevailing in Jonesville, and if the sewer is really needed in the community. Finally he goes to the chief of the division.

"Everything is approved on the Jonesville application," he says. "They have estimated the cost of the project accurately, and it will meet a very real need."

His chief signs the copy of the application and sends it back to the projects division.

In the meantime, the legal division has been conducting an equally exhaustive research. It has looked up the Jonesville charter and has found that the project is eligible for a loan and grant under Title II of the Recovery Act. It has found that Jonesville has the authority to construct the system, subject to the approval of the State Board of Health, as well as the right to put a service charge on users of the system. The lawyers determine that no election is necessary to authorize its construction. A favorable legal report is submitted to the projects division.

The finance division has concurrently been looking into the history of Jonesville to see if the city has ever defaulted on any of its bonds. It has finished the difficult job of estimating what the yearly return on the service charge for taps and bathtubs will bring the city. It has found that the charge will amply cover the loan and so the copy of the application sent to the finance division is approved and returned.

With these three approvals of the application, along with the favorable opinions of the State engineer and the chairman of the State Advisory Board, the Jonesville sewage project is on its way. As quickly as possible the application is then submitted by the Administrator with his approval to the Special Board for consideration. And the Board says:

"Yes. This is exactly in line with our policy of approving projects which improve health conditions in the communities."

Yet, after running all of these gauntlets, there is still one more approval needed—that of the man in the White House, Franklin D. Roosevelt. When this is given Jonesville is notified that an allotment for the sewage system has been made subject to certain conditions.

For a time we will detour Jonesville and its sewage system to consider some of the troubles which may arise before an application reaches the coveted goal of the Presidential signature.

Any application may fail to receive the approval of the three examining divisions, or of any one of them, and that means it cannot be submitted to the Special Board for approval. Perhaps the engineers have found that the estimated cost is too large or too small; or they may have found some flaw in the specifications. Often they refuse to approve an application because a too expensive stone is to be used on the project, or because a certain type of nails, made by a local manufacturer and not so cheap or reliable as another variety, has been specified.

Any one of a hundred legal points may stop an application. It may be that the municipality, without realizing it, does not have the right to borrow the money from the government because of its charter or on account of a limitation in the State constitution. Or it may be that the project so blithely passed by the city council must have the approval of the voters before a loan can be granted. In the same way the finance division often discovers that a city's financial history is not all written in black and so it withholds approval of the government's acceptance of bonds offered as security.

But, no matter what the reason for the disapproval, the application is sent to the Technical Board of Review for additional consideration. This body, consisting of a chairman and four to six engineers, serving on a per diem basis, is the breakwater upon which the waves of protest which follow a disapproval can beat to their hearts' content. The creation of this body was the result of nothing less than pure inspiration. Ordinarily the protests would have come right back to plague the engineer who had refused the application, or to the lawyer, or the finance man.

But the Board of Review has warded off all this trouble. It hears the complaints from the delegations, lets them argue as much as they desire, and then explains what can be done to remedy the application. In the meantime the flow of other projects has not been interrupted.

Now let us turn in again on the main road at the contracts unit of the legal division, where we left the Jonesville sewage project. Here the extremely involved work of preparing the contract between the municipality and the government is conducted. Fortunately, in the case of one sewage system, the matter is not very complicated— only fifty pages of affidavits, statements, transcripts, schedules and contracts. But in some instances, where elections have to be held before the contracts can be signed, the matter may take many weeks.

PWA has often been blamed for this unavoidable delay in starting the actual work after the money has been allocated, but the real fault has been attributable to the complicated and, in many cases, archaic, municipal laws with which our attorneys have had to cope. Or it might be that the municipality could not go ahead until the State legislature had passed an enabling act. If, for example, one of the unavoidable conditions of the allotment was that a bond election must be held, many delays that had been unforeseen, might intervene. Perhaps the local laws required publication of the election for six weeks in advance, and even after the actual election there would be another pause while the votes were being tabulated and the result announced. Even then the project might have to wait until an ordinance could be passed by the city.

These varied local and State laws and constitutional limitations which had been set up as safeguards against municipal extravagance, finally led the contracts unit to prepare model forms for each of the forty-eight States, covering all the requirements, such as elections, advertising, council approval and State authorization, which might possibly arise. But even when these forms were furnished, there were often other delays resulting from local regulations or local unfamiliarity with the forms.

For instance, bonds might be legally issued for construction, but not for demolition, yet the project might call for demolition. In such a case a guarantee must be made by the applicant, stating that the money necessary to pay for the demolition had been raised from sources other than the Federal Government.

Even after all conditions (so many there were that an addendum longer than this book would be required to list them) have been satisfied, and the applicant is given a letter of authorization to the Federal Reserve Bank, permitting an exchange of bonds for cash with which to begin construction, it is quite possible that there will be one more delay. The laws of some States make it illegal to advertise for bids and to prepare for construction before the money is actually in hand and consequently there may be a pause while the cart is being properly adjusted to the horse.

All these possible halts in the process, first between the filing of the application and the allocation of the money, and then before the start of actual construction, have caused some persons to say the whole PWA enterprise is securely bound by miles of red tape. The fact is, that considering the magnitude of its program and the lack of seasoned machinery to work with, PWA has made remarkable speed. The lack of intelligent and intelligible municipal and State laws plus, in many instances, the refusal of local officials to be hurried out of the snail's pace to which they are accustomed, have been responsible for most of the exasperating delay. Actually the technique set up by PWA has produced speed as well as safety.

We last followed the Jonesville contract into the legal department and now, because it has passed through the final stages without encountering any of the hundreds of insuperable barriers which might block the way of a less simple type of project, construction on the sewage system is about to begin.

In Jonesville nearly 400 men are employed to dig and construct the sewers because the plans call for completion within a year. They work under the more or less vigilant eyes of the local inspectors, who are employed by the city to see that cement of the proper quality is used and that the contractor does not skimp on materials. In Jonesville, perhaps, the inspectors are qualified, but in that case Jonesville may be an exception. All over the Nation the tradition of lax inspection on municipal projects is, generally speaking, religiously lived up to. In many cases the inspectors are deserving political ward heelers who would no more think of arguing with a contractor than with their alderman. Frequently their only appearances on the scene of construction are made on pay day. Many of them wouldn't know cement from taffy; or wouldn't want to.

These lax local customs called for careful Federal inspection to insure strict compliance with contracts and the maintenance of government standards. To each non-Federal project an engineer-inspector, with assistants if necessary, is assigned by the inspection division to watch the construction. He makes daily and weekly progress reports, not only on the quality of material being used, but on the number of men employed, the wages paid and the quantity of material delivered and used. He also sees that proper attention is given to accident prevention, that the men are paid promptly and according to the scale, that they are not worked too long hours, and that they are given the protection of liability insurance.

One of the outstanding accomplishments of this division was in Chicago where the sanitary district had been allotted a $41,948,000 sewage project. Poor cement was being used in one tunnel and the political inspectors of the district blithely passed the work, probably "sight unseen." Carl Bauer, the Federal engineer-inspector, warned the contractor that the quality of both work and material must be improved, but, unheeding, he continued on his way until almost 3,300 feet of rotten and dangerous tunneling had been completed. Captain Jabez Gholston of the inspection division made a special trip to Chicago to confirm his inspector's reports and then warned the district that unless it not only rejected the tunnel but renovated its inspection system the 12 million dollar grant on the gigantic project would be rescinded.

The district began to reorganize its inspection system but with such evident reluctance that it was decided to require that its men be approved by Joshua D'Esposito, resident project engineer of PWA. The sanitary district of Chicago now has a first-class group of capable and trustworthy local inspectors and exceptional work is being done on all portions of this project.

The rejected tunnel, some of which passes under railroad property and highways has now been completed to the satisfaction of our engineers. Consequently Chicago has not only avoided possible damage resulting from a defective sewer, it has cleared the path for procuring the grant for this work.

Such unaccustomed vigilance on non-Federal construction has brought us commendations from all parts of the country. Typical is a paragraph in a letter from Mr. W. W. Simmons, the architect of the building division of the Georgia State Department of Education:

"I want to state to the public and the Federal Government that in all cases we have been able to get better buildings through PWA than through any other means of schoolhouse construction."

Another such letter is that of H. G. Ripley, a prominent Massachusetts architect, who says:

"Of fundamental importance to the building industry, it seems to me, is the principle that the Federal Government is following, that a building contract, while not flexible, means the doing of no more and no less than the contract requirements."

I know that the inspection division has saved the country millions of dollars and I am convinced that it has had a wholesome influence on the building industry in every State.

At the recommendation of the Labor Advisory Board, it was decided to appoint a Board of Labor Review with three members, one representing labor, one the contractors and one the Administration. The representative of labor was not to be a member of the building trades and James Wilson, of Cincinnati, was chosen. It was stipulated that the representative of the contractors should not himself be a contractor, and so an architect, E. J. Russell, was designated to represent that group. Dr. Lindsay Rogers, of Columbia University, was selected to represent the Administration. This board has jurisdiction of all questions arising under contracts which may require adjustment. The board has functioned most successfully and so far all of its decisions have been accepted without appeal to the courts.

A most important department of PWA is the much discussed division of investigations. I realized that it would be necessary to have a check on the entire administration of the public works program, and I selected Mr. Glavis for this job.

We agreed, when we discussed the work to be done by the division of investigations, that honesty and ability were to be the only qualities considered in selecting investigators. Mr. Glavis at once organized the new force, dividing it into ten subdivisions and putting a special agent in charge of each. Three types of men were employed as agents—engineers with a thorough knowledge of construction, accountants and investigators with legal experience. A compact and thoroughly efficient force of 150 agents was finally put together. The range of these agents covers the whole field of our activity and their work has been an assurance to the country that the corruption and graft that formerly seemed inseparable from public contract work will not be tolerated under PWA.

In the purchase of land and construction materials and in dealing with labor, the crooks have found many opportunities in the past for defrauding the government. There have been some who have tried to continue this practice under PWA, but the division of investigations has been alert in its effort to uncover and bring to justice every such attempt.

Perhaps the most general offense was against the provisions assuring labor fair wages. Violations of these regulations took almost every conceivable form, from the falsification of payrolls to the so-called "kick back" by which the employer paid the prescribed wage on Saturday but on the following Monday insisted that a part of it be returned to him.

One of the many such cases was that of a firm of sub-contractors engaged on a housing project on Long Island. A carpenter complained that the contractors were demanding a "kick back" of $3.40 a day, under threat of discharge. After investigation the matter was brought to the attention of the courts. The contractors were indicted and later convicted on all charges. They were sentenced to jail and fined.

The activities of Mr. Glavis and his men have occasionally drawn a howl of surprise and anguish from some political or business crook, accustomed to the easy pickings of past public works programs, but they have the approval of the overwhelming majority of decent citizens and public servants. The people as a whole applaud our relentless war on graft and corruption. It is abhorrent to them that any one should derive a crooked or unearned profit out of public funds devoted to the welfare of the people in a time of want and distress.

Most of the description of the procedure and organization of PWA has thus far been devoted to the non-Federal part of the program, but I have not intended to slight the really important rôle played by Federal projects. It was through the different governmental departments and bureaus that we were able first to get money into circulation. Because of the fact that money was not loaned, but granted to the departments there were no legal entanglements to cut through. Moreover, the Federal departments had going organizations that could usefully spend large sums of money. They were subject only to the check of the Comptroller-General and to the approval of the Special Board. Much of their work will be discussed in later chapters.

While the major portion of the effort of the Administration has been devoted to the immediate problem of getting money into action and men into jobs, the larger problems of national planning have been considered, as provided by the Act. First the President named the National Planning Board, which, while it had no power of veto, kept track of the projects as a whole and helped to fit them into a national plan. Members of this board were Frederic A. Delano, uncle of the President, chairman, noted for his planning work in Chicago, New York, Washington and elsewhere; Charles E. Merriam, political scientist of the University of Chicago; and Wesley C. Mitchell, economist of Columbia University, with Charles W. Eliot, 2nd, acting as executive officer.

The National Planning Board, because of the magnitude of its job, worked slowly. From data prepared by it, long-range policies were developed and made available in report form. Concurrently the Mississippi Valley Committee, also an offshoot of PWA, under the chairmanship of Morris Llewellyn Cooke, of Philadelphia, formulated a plan to meet such problems as flood control, power, irrigation, soil erosion and navigation. Still other related policies were outlined by special land and mineral committees.

One of the important recommendations made by the National Planning Board in its report of June, 1934, was for a continuous national planning agency. By an executive order, President Roosevelt established the National Resources Board as successor to the National Planning Board, saying:

"The functions of the board shall be to prepare and present to the President a program and a plan of procedure dealing with the physical, social, governmental and economic aspects of public policies for the development and use of land, water and other national resources, and such related subjects as may be from time to time referred to it by the President."

This board has already presented a report that is destined to become historic, and is continuing its study of public works; of water, land and mineral uses. It has been stimulating State and regional planning through the establishment of some forty-four State planning boards, which have been set up by the governors and which are actively functioning with financial assistance from Washington.

As a result of the creation of this board and of the work it has already done and will do, the public works program of the future will be far better coördinated and integrated than any past or present program. Each dollar spent will not only return many times its value in immediate benefits through the lessening of unemployment and the supplying of some community need; it will continue to pay incalculable social dividends to generations of Americans still unborn.

Chapter IV

ROADS BRING CIVILIZATION

APPROXIMATELY one-eighth of the entire sum appropriated by Congress for the first public works program was set aside as an outright grant for road building. The 400 million dollars thus earmarked was the largest single allotment ever made by the government for highways, but the gift did not represent an entirely new attitude toward roads. Ever since 1916 the Federal policy had been to supplant the chaos of independent and unconnected road systems in the States with uniform highways integrated on a national scale, although until 1930 the States had been required to match each Federal dollar.

Just as there was no sweeping change in policy, neither did any major new effects result from the magnified road-building program. It had long been recognized that roads were particularly beneficial to the rural parts of the Nation. Wide highways offer possibilities of easier and more profitable trade for the farmers; higher standards of living for his family; greater accessibility to schools for his children. Equally clear is the relationship between good roads and the tourist—one following the other as inevitably as cause and effect. Nor is the fact novel that the construction of roads puts many men to work.

Yet, while there was no change in policy and few unanticipated effects, the very extent of PWA's road program gave to both policy and effect a unique quality.

Work for hundreds of thousands of men was, of course, the most immediate effect of the expenditure of this 400 million dollars. This figure for roads and highways became $513,914,960 by January of 1935, by which date PWA, under other sections of the Act, had greatly increased allotments for roads. In June of 1930 Federally aided road building, although even then it was a fairly comprehensive program, put 64,000 men to work. This is an impressive figure, but in June of 1934, there were 336,414 men wielding pick and shovel on streets and highways in all parts of the land.

Moreover, the work was of the best possible kind—physical labor carried on out of doors in the fresh air and sunshine. It brought a reward not only in money for poverty-stricken families, but in health for men whose bodies had suffered from lack of nourishment and whose minds had been overcast by the growing hopelessness of finding work. And, dollar for dollar, more money went for direct labor in road building than in any other kind of work.

The rapidity with which PWA was able to start the roads program was due to the efficient organization of the Bureau of Public Roads, an agency of the Department of Agriculture. This bureau, in conjunction with the highway departments of the States, had been supervising road construction in the Nation since the passage of the Federal Aid Highway Act of 1916. It already had developed a long-range program for roads, and so was able to appor-

P.W.A. IN

WASHINGTON

MONTANA

NORTH DAKOTA

IDAHO

OREGON

SOUTH DAKOTA

WYOMING

NEVADA

UTAH

NEBRASKA

CALIFORNIA

COLORADO

KANSAS

ARIZONA

NEW MEXICO

OKLA

TEXAS

Pacific Ocean

Gulf of California

OFF RELIEF ROLLS ON TO PAY ROLLS

A Map showing how the
Public Works program is Building
a Greater Nation and Making Jobs
for Men and Factories. How it
Conserves Resources and Harnesses
Rivers. How Finer Transportation
is being Created and Land Saved
for Better use.

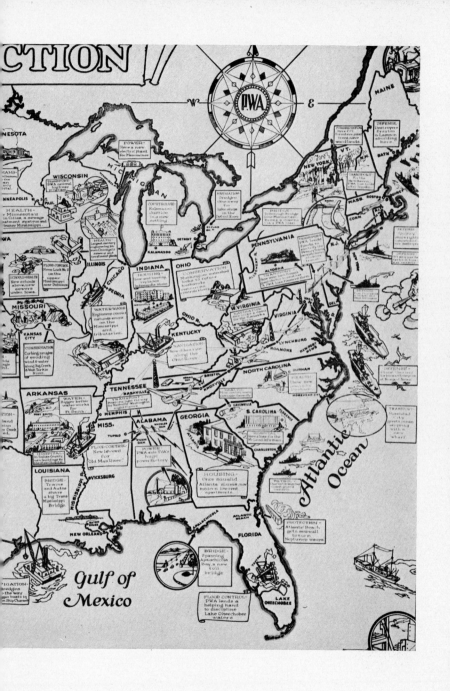

tion and start the expenditure of the 400 million dollars with a minimum of delay.

Only one major difference developed in the method of spending the money. In the past the bureau had insisted that the government funds be expended exclusively upon the main highway systems. But the National Industrial Recovery Act expressly provided that the Federal Highway Act should be amended and supplemented in order to strike at the centers of unemployment. The Special Board of Public Works, therefore, determined that not more than 50 per cent of the sum given to any State could be applied to the Federal highway system outside the corporate limits of municipalities; not less than 25 per cent to the extension of the Federal system within municipalities; and not less than 25 per cent to secondary, or feeder roads, including farm-to-market, rural free delivery and public school bus roads.

Further, it was decided to select projects according to the following priority: (a) the closing of gaps in the Federal-aid highway system; (b) the elimination of hazards to highway traffic; (c) the construction or reconstruction of projects of particular benefit or service to other agencies of the government; (d) the correlating and supplementing of existing transportation facilities by road, rail, air and water; (e) the appropriate landscaping of parkways or roadsides on a reasonably extensive mileage; (f) the reducing of maintenance costs and the decreasing of future State and local expenditures for upkeep by reconstruction of existing roads; (g) the providing of a large number of small projects designed to employ the maximum of human labor.

Each State was also required to distribute its road work through at least 75 per cent of the counties, a rule which in actual practice resulted in spreading work on the average through 86 per cent of the counties of each State.

Special care was taken by PWA to assure that as many men as possible, in proportion to the amount of money spent, would be given direct employment. Wherever it was consistent with sound economy and public advantage it was required that work be done with hand labor, rather than with machinery, but at the same time an effort was made to avoid so great an abandonment of mechanical methods as to jeopardize the road-machinery industry.

A careful study of highway construction as a means of furnishing employment for idle labor was made by the Bureau of Public Roads. It was recognized that on earth roads, where machinery plays little part in surfacing, practically all of each dollar spent goes to the laborer, but no accurate estimate had ever been made of the extent to which labor in general profits from the construction of high-type pavements, where mechanical equipment plays an important part. This study resulted in the tracing of the money paid out by States and communities for concrete pavement back through the manufacturers of equipment, repair parts, gasoline, explosives and lubricating oil to the cement and steel mills, the stone quarries and the gravel pits.

It was found that not only about ninety cents of each taxpayer's dollar was eventually paid to workers as wages and salaries, but that a very large part of the industry of the country actively shared in the work.

This of itself is adequate justification of a road-building program in a period of grave unemployment, but actually there is a more important and more permanent direct financial advantage to the country resulting from good roads. They are more economic than unimproved roads. This may seem strange, but it has been proved beyond a doubt by the interesting experiments of T. R. Agg, of the Iowa State College of Agriculture and the Mechanic Arts. Experiment and proof are reported by him as follows:

"Take a mile of typical earth road, unsurfaced. Operate over it 1,000 vehicles a day and maintain it as well as possible under that traffic for a year. The combined costs of maintaining the mile of road and operating the vehicles over it will amount to approximately $52,000 in the year, and travel will be almost impossible at certain seasons.

"Surface the same road with a *concrete* pavement. Operate over it the same traffic of 1,000 vehicles a day and maintain it under the traffic as before. Charge off the entire cost of surfacing in the life of the pavement with interest at 4 per cent and add the annual cost of the surface thus obtained to the maintenance cost. The combined costs of the mile of road and the operation of vehicles over it will amount to approximately $49,000 in the year, less by $3,000 than the cost of the earth road, and the road in this case will be in perfect condition throughout the year.

"Hence, for the traffic of 1,000 vehicles per day transportation over the concrete road costs less than over the unsurfaced earth road. For heavier traffic the difference in favor of the surfaced road is greater."

This economy of hard roads has a growing importance

in relation to our national life because each year the tourist trade becomes a greater factor in our economic system. There is scarcely anyone who does not now know the smooth feel of a finished pavement under rubber tires; the thrill of a new landscape of desert or mountain or plain; the friendliness of the Bar B-Q attendant; the comfortable yielding of a tourist-cabin bed. To millions the two oceans are no longer distant mysteries; the national parks unknown wonderlands of nature. Three million miles of roads, nearly one-third of them improved, have made all these things familiar. Upon the back of the adventurous restlessness of the American people, encouraged now for a decade by better roads and better and cheaper motor cars, rides a great new industry.

Thus upon roads (for how else can the seasonal migrations of the tourists occur except upon roads?) depends the prosperity of millions. Countless gasoline stations with their attendants; restaurants; ice-cream huts; hot-dog stands; tourist camps with their proprietors and helpers; produce stands turning crops into cash for the farmer; a thousand varieties of other stands selling everything from dolls to town lots—these are the assets of the roadside industry.

But we have not yet done with roads. Proof that they put more direct labor per dollar to healthful work than any other type of construction; that the better types are more economical in the long run than dirt roads; that they support a 3 billion dollar industry and give millions of motorists pleasure amply justifies PWA's expenditures upon them.

In the past century direct communication and transportation were supplied by the railroad. The locomotive dominated the United States. Where two railways intersected a city arose, and every line of steel tracks soon found, huddled along it, communities whose existence depended upon the service supplied by the steam-driven train. Even the mightiest industries were spiked to the heavy ties because coal was the chief source of power, and only the railroad, except in few instances, could bring coal. And with this uneven distribution of population responding to the whims or the speculative disposition of the railroader came a correspondingly uneven distribution of civilization. The cities were given much in the way of education, living comforts and luxuries; the country little.

The city man lived in his steam-heated home, with gas, electricity, modern plumbing and tap water to serve him. Stores and markets were easily available to him, and amusements, too. His children had only a few blocks to walk or ride to school. The rural man heated his home with wood, as did primitive cave peoples. He laboriously carried his water from a well which often froze in winter; lit his rooms with kerosene lamps or candles; knew of gas and electricity only by hearsay. At least three months of the year his roads were a gumbo of an unimaginable depth and consistency, so impassable as to isolate him from his nearest neighbor and to keep his children from their small and inadequate schoolhouse.

This picture is now being rapidly changed. The invention of the gasoline engine has led to the upbuilding of roads as a means of transportation and communication while the perfection of electric power and its cheaper distribution has freed industry from its dependence upon coal.

We are here concerned with the effect of roads, rather

than power, on rural sections of the Nation, but even to begin a capitulation of the benefits brought by the 20,000-odd miles of roads either built or improved under PWA would take many pages. There would be long lists of the products the farmer is now able to truck into the city on weekly or semi-weekly trips and thus take advantage of a cash market for a more varied production. There would be calculations showing how his economic status improves with the arrival of the road. There would be a section built around his wife, dealing with the savings she is able to effect by buying at lower prices in the cities, and the ease with which she is now able to secure many of the household and personal articles so necessary to a modern standard of living.

In all these things is PWA vitally interested, but their full accomplishment must be brought about by the farmer himself. He must take advantage of the new road. PWA cannot help him personally; it can only give him an opportunity.

But PWA has been able to help his children to take advantage of the roads to secure a better education. PWA had funds to spend for school buildings and for certain educational equipment, and it quickly became aware of the link between roads and a new and more desirable type of rural education. From districts where new roads were built came requests for funds for new schools. The chain of circumstances that led to this was ably explained in a letter from Leroy Martin, executive secretary of the North Carolina State School Commission, which read in part:

"The beginning of the good roads movement brought a realization to our people of the possibilities of abandoning the one- and two-teacher schools, which dotted the State in numbers exceeding 6,000 and the consequent construction of large school buildings to be used as a consolidated school and a community center.

"This began as a local project and developed as local communities became more interested in better school facilities. This program necessitated the transportation of school children upon a large scale as more and more communities worked out their plans of consolidation. At first little consideration was given to the facilities for this transportation. In many instances the parents transported their own children. It was not feasible to operate large units of transportation due to road conditions.

"With the development of the road program, which has resulted in a network of hard roads touching every community in the State, the possibilities of economies in transportation through the use of larger units became more apparent. Also the increased use of the highways by motorists made it mandatory that the pupils who were forced to ride to school must be given a safer conveyance."

Educators for many years have realized the defects of the one-room schoolhouse. In an age of increasing specialization, the teaching supplied by the rural school has yearly become less valuable because of its generalization. In the one room of the small school have been crowded pupils of different ages and different grades, all undergoing the routine instruction of a lone teacher. Because of the large number of different classes which had to be taught—at times as high as seven—she has been unable to give much time to a particular grade and none to an especially backward or unusually intelligent pupil.

And just as the pupils suffer because of the too wide-spread duties of the teacher, so does the teacher suffer from the difficulties and hardships of rural school life. She suffers from the lack of contact with other teachers and from the spiritual isolation that characterizes such a job. In order to give her pupils the same advantages that they would have if there were a teacher and a room for each class, the teacher in the one-room school would have to have at her finger tips every phase of every subject from music to algebra and from grammar to manual training.

This is not an unfair picture of the rural school, although the great number of fine men and women who in the past have received from them a fundamental education must be cited in their defense. It exemplifies, however, more of the will to learn despite obstacles than of the merits of the old system. Ideas of education have enlarged greatly since the nineteenth century when the three R's often comprised the full curriculum.

The new rural schools, made possible by good roads, are quite as modern as the best city schools. Where it was necessary to have eight one-room schools in the past, there is now a single eight-room school. The children are grouped together according to age and ability and they are taught by a teacher who is experienced in handling their particular problems and who has the time to specialize on difficult children. The larger and modern building has a marked effect upon health and attendance, and in it there is housed far superior equipment, both for education and recreation.

Moreover, the consolidated schools serve importantly

as a community center for the adult life of the area. The same rooms in which the children are taught, and the same buses, can be used to give the people of the farms an opportunity for recreational, educational and cultural activities hitherto denied them. Lastly, the consolidated schools are more economical in the end.

The money given for roads has not been the only aid the schools have received from PWA. By January 1, 1935, we had allotted approximately $137,604,560 for school construction all over the country, including the erection of new buildings, extensions on older schools, and repairs. Of this total $126,646,363 were for State, municipal and district school buildings. Construction resulting from these allotments will total $164,745,241, the difference coming from local school districts. In addition, PWA advanced $10,958,197 as outright grants to Federal educational institutions for buildings.

This helping hand by PWA will aid education in practically every part of the country and in all of its possessions. School buildings erected as part of the program dot the map from the small town of Whitefield in northern New Hampshire to Honolulu, Hawaii, and from far northern villages in Alaska to the tropical Canal Zone. In size they range from a tiny country school of the Prairie Creek Common School District in Van Zandt County, Texas, costing $2,695, to the huge $2,250,000 Bayside High School of New York City.

The amount of money asked for made no difference in our consideration of school allotments. It was our keen desire to spread the benefits of PWA to education as far as we possibly could. In addition to creating employment, causing a flow of building materials and stimulating industrial activities, it was PWA's aim to place in every part of the Nation school structures that would stand long after the program was ended as monuments to its social vision. Construction under this program includes dormitories, university classroom buildings, additions to existing buildings, new municipal or district schools, new basements, gymnasiums, auditoriums, laboratories, and swimming pools.

Moreover, PWA has also strengthened the link between schools and good roads by advancing considerable sums of money for school buses. In North Carolina, for instance, we made possible the construction of 750 school buses at a total cost of $612,000, a big step toward the complete motorization of the rural education of that State.

A summing up of the educator's opinion of the aid given all types of education by PWA is contained in a letter from Raymond V. Long, director of school buildings for the Virginia State Board of Education. He wrote:

>   Commonwealth of Virginia,
>   State Board of Education,
>   Richmond.

My DEAR MR. SECRETARY:

On behalf of the public schools and institutions of higher learning in Virginia, may we offer our sincere appreciation to the Public Works Administration for the outstanding opportunity it has offered the public schools and educational institutions in Virginia to improve our physical plants under the Public Works Program.

The results in brief accruing from this program may be summarized in:

(a) A realization of a building program contemplated in many cases for years that could not have been accomplished under the normal tax incomes and public appropriations.

(b) An inspired demand in isolated rural communities for a far superior quality of construction than that which they have been accustomed to, which improved construction we think is largely attributable to encouragement for such improved construction under the Public Works Program.

(c) In arousing a demand for improved school plant facilities, which a recent survey just being completed indicates will call for an expenditure of $8,000,000 to $10,000,000 within the next five years to meet actual school building needs.

(d) In very definitely setting up a greatly improved standard of ethics and procedure in the construction industry that is seriously needed, and will no doubt permanently affect the construction industry.

(e) The broad underlying principles back of the Public Works Program have of course emanated from those in responsible charge of administering the program, and the administration of these principles has on the whole been eminently satisfactory. While some mistakes have been made by many of us in the discharge of administrative details, yet these mistakes are of minor consequences, and will soon be forgotten, while all the really worthwhile principles involved will carry on and affect permanently, we hope, the whole public improvement program.

Permit me, therefore, on behalf of the public schools and the institutions of higher learning governing bodies to express to you our genuine and sincere appreciation in Virginia for the very magnificent results that have accrued to us from the Public Works Program, and the hope that during the next year it may be possible to continue a somewhat similar program that may bring even more far-reaching results.

Good roads have been an increasing help to rural districts in another way. A great many counties have been distributing books by bus to isolated homes and farmers have been coming in to the libraries in greater numbers.

As a result, there has been a demand for larger and improved library buildings. By January 1, 1935, $1,824,100 of PWA funds had been allotted either to build or to make addition to eighteen libraries.

Hospitals, too, have become more available to country families as the result of the new roads. Not only can doctors and nurses reach rural patients more easily, but serious cases can be taken with much less trouble to the medical centers. In the past the doctor was often forced to abandon his automobile and travel either by horseback or on foot to reach an isolated case. Frequently, because of this primitive method of travel, he arrived too late, and even when he reached the bedside in time he might be forced to improvise surgical instruments from household utensils for an emergency operation because he did not dare to run the risk of transporting his patient to the nearest hospital over bad roads.

This situation has now changed in many parts of the country. The hospitals are caring for a larger number of rural patients. This new demand upon them has resulted in a need for greater facilities, to meet which PWA has been happy to provide them with financial assistance. The allotments for hospital projects on January 1, 1935, amounted to $56,243,644. This money was for the construction of new buildings, extensions of existing buildings, laundries and nurses' homes. In some cases aid was given to modernize hospitals, the money going for heating systems, refrigerating plants, etc.

Not so directly connected with roads, although their members have done much work improving and beautifying our highways, are the camps of the Civilian Conservation

Corps, one of PWA's greatest contributions to the improvement of rural life. These camps, with their companies of healthy young men between 18 and 25, however, are far more than tools with which to landscape the Nation. We like to think of them as rescue stations for a generation which came very near being permanently undone by the depression.

Even if there had not been a need for all sorts of useful work in national and State parks, on the public domain and in the Nation's forest lands, these CCC camps could easily have justified themselves merely as agencies for social regeneration. Everyone remembers, back in the gloomy, depression-misted days of 1930-1932, the faces of youths begging for dimes on the street corners of any community. Pale and hopeless most of these faces were, and often pinched with hunger. The adventurous among them thumbed their luckless way back and forth across the continent. Freight trains carried quotas of them from city to city; a doorway or a railroad culvert served as a shelter for them from rain and sleet; the bread lines were extended to encompass their youthful and tragically undernourished figures. Those of us who halted to talk with them discovered many were high school, even college, graduates; found that most of them knew one or more trades by which they could earn a living if the opportunity offered.

But there was no opportunity. Millions of their elders, better trained, physically stronger, were out of work. The Nation was placarded with a gigantic "No Help Wanted" sign. And that was what hurt them most, not the sickness and the hunger, but the sign. They weren't wanted.

Then, suddenly, in March of 1933, President Roosevelt created the Civilian Conservation Corps, to be supervised in its various branches by the Departments of War, Interior, Agriculture and Labor. The Department of Labor was given the job of selecting, through the various relief agencies, young men who were unemployed and whose families were dependent upon charity. The army, assigned to mobilize, equip, transport and house them, received those men at a rate of 8,500 a day—a mobilization rate exceeding the combined records of the army and navy in the World War.

Enlistments were at first for six months, and by June 7, a large number of the million men who were to pass through nearly 1,600 camps from Maine to Oregon were in conditioning quarters. To one of these camps the President, speaking on the spiritual values to be derived from the corps, said:

"Through you the Nation will graduate a fine group of strong young men, clean living, trained to self-discipline and, above all, willing and proud to work for the joy of working."

The men, upon being accepted for enlistment, agreed to send $20 to $25 of their $30 monthly pay home to dependents. They were given food, clothing, shelter and medical care, and in return they were required to work forty hours each week, practically every minute of it out of doors.

Moreover, the work they did, and are doing is valuable. This was not just a gesture to their pride on the part of Uncle Sam designed to take the sting out of giving them a dole. As soon as their city eyes became accustomed to the strange and exciting scenery of forests and national parks they saw the importance of what they were doing. On every side were visible the scars caused by past extravagant and wasteful handling of our once vast timber lands, and they quickly saw the newer traces of losses from erosion, forest fires, insects and tree diseases which have cost the Nation more than half a billion dollars a year.

It is to the great credit of the men that the hopelessness engendered by their futile search for jobs was so quickly banished by the realization that they were really needed by the Nation. They fell to work with a will and accomplished results which would have shamed an ordinary army of manual workers.

While sixty classifications of work have been performed by the CCC, the bulk of their efforts has been directed toward fireproofing the Nation's timbered areas and, in addition, protecting the forests and parks from tree-attacking insects, diseases and other forest menaces. Special emphasis has been placed upon the correction and prevention of soil erosion.

Some of the major items of work completed by the men by December of 1934, as listed by Robert E. Fechner, director of emergency conservation work, include much fire fighting, the construction of 41,000 miles of truck roads to facilitate the movements of fire-fighting units, the building of 1,200 lookout houses and towers, and the erection of 25,000 miles of telephone lines. Over 5 million acres of land the corps conducted rodent control operations; they planted more than 200 million trees to halt soil erosion and improve forests; they carried out great campaigns to control tree diseases; and they completed nearly one million soil-erosion prevention dams.

The present money value of this work, as reported by

the Departments of War, Interior and Agriculture, on January 1, 1935, totaled $291,688,433, but the real return to the country will come much later when timber production and forest resources, now falling off dangerously, will show a decided increase. Some day, I have no doubt, the work of the CCC will be considered the prime factor in the salvaging of America's forests and public domain.

It would be impossible to calculate in dollars the physical, mental and spiritual values accruing to these men from their work. We know that practically one in every ten young unmarried men in the country has passed through the camps and returned to his home a changed individual. These young men were stronger; their backs were straighter, their eyes clearer, their minds more alert; they were healthy. Many of them had formed new health habits under the medical supervision of the camps. They had learned the value of discipline and the art of working with their fellow men. They had developed self-respect and a sense of responsibility.

They had become good citizens.

Chapter V

WATER IS WEALTH

STUMBLING over rocks and clods of baked earth, oxen pulled on the top-heavy wagons of the long Mormon train. Beside the animals walked the bearded elders of the church, their eyes searching vainly for the lush meadows and the green trees of the promised land. The sun that burned their faces flashed alluring mirages in the lavender haze that lay over the sage brush. From the lurching vehicles came the voices of women and children, hushed because their leader, Brigham Young, lay ill in his own covered wagon. Ahead, on either side, and back of them lay friable alkali soil, rocks, brush and jagged mountains.

Suddenly the caravan halted and Erastus Snow, out in front of the others, was touched on the arm. "Brother Young wants you," a boy informed him.

Snow joined a group of the elders behind Brigham Young's wagon. Presently the leader appeared before them and said:

"Bear ye to the north and soon ye will find a nice stream of water, and there ye are to throw up a dam and plow the land and plant potatoes and seeds as quickly as possible."

The train was promptly swung to the north and, as their

leader had said, they encountered a stream. It came down from the mountain, clear and cold.

So began the first irrigation project conducted by Anglo-Saxons in America; but others followed. Water unlocked the fertility imprisoned in the barren land and presently the Mormons had thousands of crop-producing acres in the Salt Lake Valley. Yet even Brigham Young's vision probably did not foretell the millions of persons whose existence nearly a hundred years later would depend upon the wise use of river water.

And those millions cause a new water problem which, in Utah at least, is more acute than it was in the days of the Mormon pioneers. Like many another natural resource of America, the once more than abundant water has become insufficient for the State. There is not enough to go around.

Almost the entire West is facing a similar problem because in the last twenty years agriculture has become its major industry. The economic collapse of that section, threatened by the sharp decline in mining and lumbering, was averted by the growth of irrigation farming.

Utah, the same territory which Brigham Young's followers found so fertile, furnishes the best illustration of what lack of adequate water reserves means to the West's growing dependence upon the soil. The story of a single farmer will pose the problem—and PWA's solution of it.

The farmer is John Smith, of Weber County, Utah. He is fifty-five years old, and has spent all his life on the plot selected as irrigable land ninety years ago by his great-grandfather. In the prosperous days of the very recent past, when there was sufficient water, Smith has often rested for a moment on his ditch hoe, his rubber boots ankle deep in rich mud, and peered at the blue-misted Wasatch Mountains thankfully. In his heart there was a feeling of gratitude that his great-grandfather had had the foresight to homestead close to the mountain range and to the Ogden River, so that in July, August and September the water from the natural reservoir in the hills could be used to flood his sun-baked acres.

The history of irrigation development in John Smith's territory is typical of Utah, and for that matter, of the West. The pioneers would cut a channel in the stream bank to divert water onto adjacent lands. This was quite a simple thing to do. But neighbors came and a system had to be worked out whereby one man would not get all of the water. Diversion works, which could be opened and closed at will, were built, and finally, with the arrival of still more settlers, and with all of the water in the stream utilized there was still an unsatisfied demand for more.

The flow in John Smith's stream had distinct seasonal fluctuations. There were spring freshets from snow melting in the mountains and, at times in summer, rain in the same regions brought a flood of one or two days' duration. It became obvious, about the time Smith's grandfather succeeded to the farm, that this excess water must be stored for use in the periods when the supply was low.

At first the settlers stored water in the sloughs and in small waterholes for service during the dry months, and later groups of them built small dams. But as Salt Lake City and Ogden increased in population and the demand for vegetables, meat and fruit became ever greater, more land was tilled, until the water reserves became insufficient to meet the demands made upon them. A contributing factor was the necessity of maintaining a special reserve of water, which ordinarily would have been employed in irrigation, for the use of the urban population.

After 1920 the problem became acute. John Smith's farm was plowed faithfully in the spring, but a part of his crops, indeed often the greater part, always failed for lack of water. Where his father had harvested three crops of alfalfa a season, he was fortunate to harvest one. Likewise, his other crops—sugar beets, vegetables and fruit, were poor in quality and of insufficient quantity.

The economic pinches resulting from the scarcity of water were felt not alone by John Smith and the other Utah wet farmers. True it is that they began to experience poverty, but the big Utah cities and the rest of the country also suffered ill effects from the same cause. Salt Lake City and Ogden were forced to import farm products from other sections of the country at a considerable rise in cost and consumers were required to pay higher prices for the necessities of the table. At the same time the manufacturers of the Middle West and the East, the producers of motor cars, of textiles and of shoes, felt a slackening in the demand for goods from these farmers who were no longer prosperous.

The answer to John Smith's problem, from an engineering standpoint, was fairly simple. It was known that the existing irrigated farms located along his stream, as well as along most of the others, made a pretty complete use of the summer flow. The supply of additional water therefore must come from the storage of the flood waters and of the unused summer flow. It followed that reservoirs would be necessary to impound these waters and to regulate their flow from one season to another, or even over a series of several years. Experts agreed that it would not be a complicated job to build such reservoirs.

Necessity and opportunity united to give birth to the reclamation policy of the United States by virtue of which great impounding dams have arisen in various sections to hold and conserve precious waters for use on arid but fertile lands that are capable of producing abundant crops of many varieties. Coöperating groups of farmers, under the leadership of the Bureau of Reclamation and with the aid of money advanced by the United States, to be repaid under the law over a term of years, have happily transformed desert places into veritable garden spots while at the same time aiding in a vital way in the economic upbuilding of a vast empire that, without reclamation, would be left largely to produce sage brush to furnish shade to jack rabbits.

Reclamation had long been a fixed and important policy of government when PWA came into being. Naturally, the West wanted to share in its benefits in order to create new reclamation districts and to improve existing projects. But there were complications. In order to obtain PWA funds, the farmers in the various districts had to organize water-users' associations so that they would have the power to contract with the Federal Government, and to guarantee repayment of the project costs. Many meetings were held while the farmers discussed the advisability of entering into a coöperative obligation to build and pay for works far larger than any of which they theretofore had dreamed.

Simultaneously, the Utah Water Storage Commission

and the Bureau of Reclamation of the Interior Department, under Dr. Elwood Mead, commissioner, were busy correlating the purely local projects of the farmers into a comprehensive State plan. Each stream system was first looked upon as a unit available to serve the needs of the community most intimately concerned, and then studied with reference to its place in a larger plan. In developing individual project plans to a point where they could be approved, it was necessary to consider the factors of water supply, land productivity, markets, agricultural economics, engineering feasibility, social desirability, the cost to the individual farmer and his ability to pay.

The adoption of the final project plans involved considerable surveying of engineering features and the testing and exploration of many dam sites. The investigation and the working out of the project plans and most of the organization details were accomplished by a field organization located at Salt Lake City under the direction of the commissioner and the chief engineer of the Bureau of Reclamation.

The most interesting of the projects was decided upon by the engineers because of a possible future lack of water in the immediate neighborhood of Salt Lake City. It called for the construction of a five and one-half mile tunnel through the Wasatch Mountains from the Duchesne River to the Provo River, which would cause the water from the Duchesne, which ordinarily runs into the Colorado River, to reverse its course and travel almost backward toward Salt Lake.

Finally, five main projects, costing 16 million dollars, were approved, and a PWA allocation was made for them. Included in the general plan are four large dams, several important canals and other engineering works too extensive and expensive for the people to undertake privately. These projects are briefly outlined as follows:

Hyrum Project

Includes the Hyrum Dam (earthfill 90 feet high) and three small distributing canals. The reservoir will have a live storage capacity of 14,000 acre feet, and with natural flow diversions will furnish water for 12,000 acres of land already being farmed.

Construction was started March 20, 1934, and will be completed during the summer of 1935. The estimated cost of the project is $930,000.

Ogden River Project

Includes the Pineview Dam (earth and rockfill 80 feet high) a 5.2 mile pipe-line, and two distributing canals with a length of 31 miles. The Pineview Reservoir will have a capacity of 38,000 acre feet and will furnish a supplemental water supply to a highly developed agricultural area of 20,000 acres adjacent to Ogden and Brigham City.

Construction was started in December, 1934, and will be completed some time in 1936. The estimated cost of the project is $3,000,000.

Moon Lake Project

Includes the Moon Lake Dam (earthfill 90 feet high), two feeder canals 38 miles long connecting three small rivers, and possibly one small storage reservoir. The Moon Lake Reservoir will have a capacity of 30,000 acre feet and the small reservoir 5,000 acre feet. The storage water from these reservoirs, together with the diversion of surplus water to be made available through the construction of the feeder canals, will supplement the present water supply on about 65,000 acres under existing canal systems.

Construction was recently started on this project, and will be completed during 1936, or early in 1937. The estimated cost of the project is $1,500,000.

Sanpete Project

Consists of two tunnels, with collecting ditches near the headwaters of the San Rafael River, to divert surplus water from the Green River watershed to supplement the irrigation supply in the Great Salt Lake Basin near the towns of Ephraim and Spring City in Sanpete County. The Ephraim and Spring City tunnels will be 1½ miles and one mile long, respectively. About 13,000 acres of land already under irrigation will be benefited.

Construction will be started on the tunnels in the spring of 1935, and, in all probability, will be completed by the end of 1936. The estimated cost of the project is $300,000.

Provo River Project

Construction features include the Deer Creek Dam (earth and rockfill, 200 feet high); a 5½ mile tunnel for the diversion of surplus water from the Green River Basin to the Great Salt Lake Basin; enlargement of the nine-mile Weber-Provo canal connecting the Weber and Provo rivers; one distributing canal 22 miles long; relocations of the railroad and highway; a 5½ mile dike (earth and rockfill, 23 feet high) across the south end of Utah Lake for the purpose of reducing the water-surface area and evaporation; and the revision of the present Jordan River outlet from Utah Lake.

The Deer Creek Reservoir will have a live storage capacity of 160,000 acre feet. The average saving of evaporation from Utah Lake by diking will be about 60,000 acre feet annually. The reservoir water and the water saved from evaporation will benefit about 95,000 acres of irrigated lands in Utah and Salt Lake Counties. The estimated cost of the entire project is approximately $10,000,000.

The project, which involves many difficulties and problems in organization, is expected to be started during the summer of 1935.

The present irrigation difficulties in Utah are due to excessive demands on the available water supply. These demands were aggravated during the three years' period prior to 1935 by an abnormally low rainfall. It became evident that the farmers in most of the over-developed areas could not remain there much longer without an additional water supply.

The five projects enumerated are of immense value to Utah, which depends fundamentally upon the products of the soil for its prosperity. The establishment of water reserves for the 205,000 acres already being farmed in Utah will make for self-sustaining agriculture, directly benefiting more than one-fourth of the population of the State and indirectly benefiting the remainder.

For man's economic use of water—reclamation and irrigation projects as in Utah, navigation projects, flood-control projects and power projects—PWA has contributed about 500 million dollars. The largest of the allotments was made to the corps of engineers of the War Department. The grants made to the engineers, who have been in charge of America's rivers and harbors for more than one hundred years, amounted to $344,607,753. Most of this sum was for navigation and flood-control projects, the largest of which are the Fort Peck Dam on the upper Missouri, Bonneville Dam on the Columbia River, and the upper Mississippi improvement program.

To the Tennessee Valley Authority went 50 million dollars for the spectacular development in the valley of the Tennessee River, outstanding features of which I shall discuss in a later chapter. The remaining 105-odd million dollars, because it was intended largely for irrigation, was assigned to the Bureau of Reclamation in the Department of the Interior. However, to complete the projects approved will require an additional 123 millions.

Although this money was divided among various organizations, it would be a mistake to think that the work being done with water is not a part of a general plan. The government is not proceeding in a haphazard manner. It is undertaking no projects without reference both to their special and their general relationship to our national program. We are all working together for a unified and intelligent development instead of unheedingly establishing small and unrelated projects. Under the President's direct leadership, the plans of the War Department for flood control and navigation, the work of my own Interior Department in reclamation and soil erosion, the projects of TVA, and the endeavors of the forest service of the Department of Agriculture have all been united along a single front.

To Theodore Roosevelt, who founded the Bureau of Reclamation, the word meant simply giving fertile lands an opportunity to bear crops and life by making water available. Irrigated tracts produced new farms, homesteads and unfailing crops, for which there were ready markets. In his time there were no such questions as agricultural overproduction, glutted markets and an undisposable export surplus.

Today, reclamation is a vast and vexing problem. The Administration of Franklin D. Roosevelt must proceed carefully in placing new land under cultivation. Indeed, one of its major concerns is to discourage the accumulation of surplus foodstuffs which cannot be sold either here or abroad. We have had to adopt an entirely different policy from that of former years. We have found that reclamation, as we knew it in the past, is only one piece of a jig-saw puzzle that must be fitted into the national picture. We know that we must move in an orderly and reasonable way. To that end we are studying the Nation's resources in their entirety; we are trying to coördinate them into an efficient social and economic unit. We no longer view great rivers and watersheds in the light of what a particular locality thinks it wants. Having in mind the principle of the greatest good for the greatest number of our citizens, we are exploring our water resources everywhere with our minds on cheaper sources of power, better facilities for navigation and the salvaging of our good earth from the plundering of uncontrolled wind and water.

We do not now consider it good policy to build an isolated and unrelated irrigation dam in order to impound waters for the benefit of a small area. The present status of reclamation work in the United States negatives any charge that we are pursuing a blind policy. The Bureau of Reclamation is not devoted mainly to bringing fresh lands into cultivation; it is a rescue agency for lands already being farmed. Reservoirs already built have saved the civilization of many important Western communities. With allotments from PWA, the bureau is building seventeen reservoirs in eleven States, as well as completing canals, all of which will supplement the scanty water supply of a score of drought-stricken territories.

As has already been said, reclamation has been the chief factor in averting the economic collapse of the West. As an example, in 1900 the gold and silver output of Colorado was about 50 million dollars; in 1930 it had shrunk to 6 million dollars. The processions of ore trains that once came out of the canyons of Boulder and Clear Creeks and the Platte and Arkansas rivers are gone. What was once the leading railroad from Denver to Leadville has been abandoned. If there had been no other resource to take the place of the worked-out mines, if some profitable employment for labor could not have been found, Denver to-day would be another "Hoover" city with grass growing in its streets, as it does in Leadville and Cripple Creek. The resource that was available was the water of its streams, replenished from the snows of its mountain summits, making fertile the wonderful soil of the valleys. To-day the irrigated farms of Colorado give employment to more people and yield more certain and larger returns than the mines ever did. Nor is Colorado the only instance of the kind. Boise, Idaho; Phœnix, Arizona; Yakima, Washington, are other examples of prosperous transitions from other industries to irrigated farming.

The dependability of irrigation farming was again demonstrated during the drought of the summer of 1934. Farmland banks and local real-estate offices in the Yakima reclamation area in the State of Washington received floods of inquiries from farmers in the drought-stricken sections, requesting information on homesteading possibilities. Many farmers went directly to the region with equipment and cash, seeking opportunities to establish themselves on the fertile well-watered lands. Even reclamation projects located in the sections ravaged by last year's disastrous drought had an assured water supply. These regions, along with the surrounding territory, went without rain for months. The rivers dried up. But because of their storage reservoirs the water ran plentifully through the ditches and crops and the irrigated land throve.

In the early days of reclamation opportunities to generate hydro-electric power as a co-product were disregarded, both in the construction of the dams and in the reclamation laws. Now the possibility of generating such power is one of the important factors in determining the desirability of new works. The value of power plants is twofold. Life on the farm is made easier, the electric washer and the electrically driven cream separator saving many a weary arm and tired back. Moreover, the revenue from several of the power plants already built is greater than the income received from the irrigators. This income lightens the financial load of the farmers and makes possible many projects, which, without it, would not be feasible.

It is doubtful if the great development to control and utilize the Colorado River at Black Canyon would ever have been approved by Congress had it not been for the fact that contracts for the power to be generated there insure the repayment in fifty years, with interest at four per cent, of all the money spent by the government on the project. The increased use of hydro-electric power has brought hope to the farmers in the Imperial Valley. Here there were times when no water at all was available; when water for domestic purposes and livestock had to be shipped in by train. There was always the danger that the

10,000 acres of citrus fruit orchards would be killed. As it was there was a crop loss of 9 million dollars in 1934. But the people who saw their crops shrivel up held on because they knew that Boulder Dam was being built and that its great reservoir would put an end to fears of drought.

When a swirl of muddy water formed at the base of this gigantic structure on February 1, 1935, the last chapter in the story of a construction achievement which now ranks as the first man-made wonder of the world, was begun. Almost twice as high as the next highest dam, the 726-foot structure dwarfs the pyramids of Egypt and towers above all but a few modern skyscrapers. It is, by far, the most sensational of all reclamation enterprises.

The history of Boulder Dam extends back to 1895 when the first attempt was made to harness the powerful Colorado. Some enterprising men built comparatively small diversion works near the river's delta, thereby securing water to irrigate a part of Imperial Valley, but in ten years a flood, by destroying 8 million dollars' worth of property and crops, demonstrated the inadequacy of this undertaking. Later, Theodore Roosevelt ordered that a survey be made by engineers of the river's irrigation possibilities. The result of the report that was made was Boulder Dam—twenty-five years after.

For this project, including the All-American Canal, PWA has thus far allocated 47 million dollars, in addition to more than 56 million dollars appropriated for the dam by Congress at different times.

When, on July 3, 1930, Congress passed the initial appropriation for the dam, preliminary construction work

Boulder Dam. Night and day work made possible by a PWA allotment brought this vast dam to completion two and one-half years ahead of schedule.

was started at once. Over a railroad that stretched between Las Vegas, Nevada, and the Boulder Dam site began to pour the greatest volume of freight ever hauled to a single engineering project. From the factories of the East came reinforcing steel, pipes, gates and valves, structural steel and machinery. From the West came lumber. Contracts for cement were awarded to widely separated plants in all parts of the country. Thousands of barrels were used daily.

Indeed, when the last 20-ton bucket of concrete was poured into the dam on February 22, 1935, the railroad had brought in enough of this material to have built a monument 100 feet square to a height of two and one-eighth miles, or to have built a standard paved road from Miami to Seattle.

The concrete wall of the dam weighs 6,600,000 tons, and the section at the bottom, which is 660 feet thick, will easily withstand water pressure which, when the 115-mile reservoir is filled in 1939, is expected to amount to 45,000 pounds to the square foot. Due to the tremendous weight of the concrete itself, and the high temperatures in the area when it was poured, heat of 150 degrees Fahrenheit was generated within the walls and would have prevented the concrete from hardening if 570 miles of steel tubing, through which ice water was pumped, had not been laced through the entire structure. Even with this artificial cooling system it will take two years for the concrete to set, but without it, according to engineers, the cooling would have required 150 years.

Six miles to the west of the dam site, high on the arid sands, a model city of Spanish architecture sprang up to house the thousands of workers. Homes, mess halls, a hospital, club-house, machine shop, garage, laundry and schools were raised almost over night. For unmarried workers twelve great dormitories were built and equipped in the most modern fashion with air-conditioning systems, running water and shower baths. Streets and sidewalks were laid out, a sewage system was installed. A city planner was employed to keep the new community attractive and efficient, and in approximately one year the third largest city in Nevada was completed and functioning under a city manager form of government.

In the Boulder City workshops the engineers planned and constructed outlet pipe sections too large to be shipped from distant points. In laboratories thousands of feet of X-ray pictures were developed so that any defects in the welding work could be detected.

The dam itself progressed at the rate of a foot a day. The work of the "Six Companies," the contracting corporations which combined to undertake the contract, went smoothly and rapidly. Near the end of the job the work was speeded up to the maximum. Three shifts of men, working eight hours each, were employed and construction was pushed at night under brilliant electric light.

The contractors had agreed to finish not later than January 1, 1938, or to pay a forfeit of nine thousand dollars for each day's delay, but instead of paying damages they earned a bonus. As the result of extraordinary activity the work was actually completed two and a half years ahead of schedule, thus assuring the government additional revenue from the power plant and saving a substantial amount in interest on the capital expended.

Figures which attempt to portray the size of the dam or the amount of water impounded by it are difficult to grasp. The project's immensity may only be grasped properly by a trip to the Black Canyon, a walk below the towering wall on the down river side, and a drive in an automobile over the 45-foot paved highway on the top of the dam. The size of the reservoir is as hard to describe. It will be 115 miles long; it will provide refuge for wild life and fish; it will contain, when it is full, as it will be in about four years, enough water to flood New York State to a depth of one foot, enough to provide every person on earth with 5,000 gallons, or each person in the United States with 80,000 gallons. But it must be seen to be appreciated.

When the entire Boulder Dam project is completed it will have cost 147 million dollars exclusive of interest during construction. There must still be appropriated about 60 million dollars, most of which will be used for power development and the construction of the All-American Canal from the Colorado River to the Imperial and Coachella Valleys in southeastern California. The canal will cost $38,500,000, and will pay for itself over a period of years.

Water for drinking purposes will be furnished through the canal to San Diego, California, and to Los Angeles, through a 200 million dollar aqueduct now under construction. Electric power will be supplied to the city of Los Angeles and others from the estimated continuous firm power output of 663,000 horsepower. Irrigation water will go to the 600,000 acres now being tilled in California and to the 60,000 acres under cultivation in Arizona. Another million acres of irrigable land, almost equally divided between California and Arizona, will be available for homesteading as soon as it is considered advisable to put them under cultivation.

As a rule it has not been the policy of PWA to finance new reclamation projects. In most cases, as in Utah, the money that has been expended on such enterprises has been used to aid lands already reclaimed, but endangered by a too scant or a failing water supply. There have been a few exceptions to this rule which I will discuss.

We allocated funds to complete the Owyhee and Vale projects in Oregon, which were started seven years ago, and for the Sun River project in Montana, where construction began in 1916. We would not have undertaken these as new enterprises at this time, but it seemed economically sound and socially justified to finish them. We approved an important project for the Verde River in Arizona, but we rescinded the allocation when the Bureau of Reclamation reported that the cost was too high to warrant the expenditure. I especially cite this fact because it refutes reckless statements that we have not given sufficient thought to engineering and financial factors in undertaking reclamation projects.

The Casper-Alcova project in Wyoming will admittedly bring in 66,000 new acres, but the principal crop will be alfalfa hay and other forage products for the winter feeding of live stock. Wyoming cattlemen have found for years that drought conditions on their range are frequently so severe that they cannot winter their herds at home. They have had to drive them as far south as the Texas Panhandle. Besides entailing great cost, which the consumer eventually pays in higher prices for meat, this has meant the loss of many head of cattle. Another justification for Casper-Alcova is the production of cheap power for which there is a clamorous market within reasonable distance of the proposed dam.

The people of Natrona County, where this project lies, have an especial claim for consideration, as does the whole West generally with respect to expenditures for reclamation purposes. Natrona County has contributed more than 30 million dollars to the reclamation fund from oil royalties, and its people feel that the State is entitled to some share of this money in order to add to the permanent welfare of the community. Teapot Dome, which a few years ago added to the prosperity of certain gentlemen, although it tarnished their reputations, lies in this same county.

Another record-breaking reclamation-power project is in course of construction as a PWA project on the Columbia River, about 70 miles west of Spokane, Washington. This is the Grand Coulee Dam, for which a present allocation of 63 million dollars has been made. The original application called for a dam of the height of 500 feet, at a cost of $181,101,000. It is interesting to remember, in this connection, that the cost of Boulder Dam and power plant, when completed, will be 109 million dollars. Since it was feasible to build a lower dam at Grand Coulee which could later be increased in height, PWA decided to authorize a structure of 297 feet.

That the higher dam will ultimately be built can hardly be doubted by anyone who has visited this site and who has made even a cursory survey of the magnitude and the richness of the now desert land that, once water is turned on to it, could be organized into farms that would yield abundant and varied crops to happy and prosperous farmers. No less than 1,200,000 acres of such land could be irrigated with the water capable of being impounded by the high dam.

Considered as a power project, it is interesting to note that the low dam will generate 420,000 K.W., while the high dam would produce 1,280,000 K.W. at a cost per kilowatt hour of two mills for firm power. The low dam will form a reservoir 75 miles in length and the high dam one of 150 miles. To complete the high dam, if it is authorized before the completion of the present project, would require five years. The low dam will be finished in three and a half to four years.

Some comparisons between the high dam at Grand Coulee and Boulder Dam will be interesting. Boulder has risen to a height of 730 feet, while Grand Coulee, when completed, will be 500 feet high. The crest length of Boulder is 1,180 feet and Grand Coulee will be 4,000 feet. Three million two hundred and fifty thousand cubic yards of concrete have been used in building Boulder Dam, but this is dwarfed by the 11 million cubic yards that will go into the high Grand Coulee Dam and thus establish a new world's record. The power-plant capacity of Boulder will be 1,835,000 horsepower as against 2,520,000 for Grand Coulee, while the generating units (Kilovolt-ampere) will rate as follows: 82,500 for Boulder and 105,000 for Grand Coulee.

Although they are not intended primarily for irrigation, the army's chief water projects are almost as spectacular as some of the great reclamation projects. An-

The Mississippi River work of the Public Works Administration will leave the Nation with a heritage of long-sought dams and navigation aids which will go a long way toward restoring river traffic to a place of great importance in the economic life of the Mississippi Valley. The work is under the supervision of the Corps of Engineers, to which the allotment of $94,500,000 was made. This picture shows a general view of Lock No. 7 looking north at Dresbach, Minnesota.

other Columbia River undertaking to which PWA has allotted more than 30 million dollars, is the Bonneville Dam, forty miles from Portland, Oregon. This dam will provide water for irrigation, it will make the Columbia River navigable to the Snake River, it will aid flood and soil erosion control, and it will bring, through the generation of cheap power, an increased development to the Northwest. An interesting feature of this dam will be the construction of giant fishways, for which the sum of $3,200,000 has been provided, as an aid to the salmon to scale the 54-foot dam when they feel the urge to go to the upper stretches of the river on their honeymoons.

In order to provide water all the year round for navigation on the Missouri River, and to prevent floods, a huge reservoir dam is being constructed by the army engineers at Fort Peck in eastern Montana. When the project is completed, at an expenditure of 50 million dollars from PWA, a lake 175 miles long will have been created. Also in the interest of navigation is the Upper Mississippi Project, which includes the construction of many locks and the dredging of a nine-foot channel from Minneapolis to St. Louis. PWA has given 51 million 495 thousand dollars for this work.

As obviously beneficial to the country as all of these projects are, there has been certain criticism directed at them. The charges of those opposed to governmental development of the Nation's power reserves I shall take up in the next chapter. But aside from this opposition, many misinformed people in the industrial East have complained bitterly that a large part of their taxes is diverted to pay for irrigation benefits for the West.

This is a misapprehension. The original funds for reclamation were derived from the sale of public lands in the Western States. Subsequently Congress provided that a major share of oil royalties, which accrue entirely in the West, should go into a revolving fund for reclamation purposes. Not only are the reclamation projects financed by the West, but in the course of time the whole cost of construction and maintenance returns to the Federal treasury. They are self-liquidating. The money that the farmers pay for the water and power they use goes back into a revolving fund. Water users have already repaid 49 million dollars and power revenues have added another six and one-half million. All reclamation projects, by law, are on this self-sustaining basis.

Moreover, the rest of the country receives direct benefits from the markets which these areas create for manufacturers, merchants and carriers. A recent survey revealed that in one year 95,000 carloads of manufactured goods valued at 120 million dollars were shipped to points in seventeen of these reclaimed places. Although Boulder Dam lies in the basin of the Colorado River between Nevada and Arizona, many of the millions of dollars spent there have gone into the tills of manufacturers at Schenectady, Pittsburgh, Gary, Youngstown, Birmingham and other eastern industrial centers.

This, then, is the past, present and future status of reclamation. I have discussed it somewhat fully in the hope that I might be able to dispel the mistaken but frequently heard suggestion that Eastern taxpayers are forced to pay tribute in order to build up the sparsely settled regions in the West.

There is another prevalent notion that is equally erroneous and that is that we should not develop and utilize our natural blessings in an orderly and reasonable manner. I cherish the hope that a frank statement of the facts may serve to prevent the growth of a sectional or partisan prejudice on this important question at a time when we are embarking on the most worth-while task of empire saving and building that the world has witnessed in ancient or modern times.

CHAPTER VI

CHEAP POWER

At the present time the greatest potential source of national wealth lies undeveloped in our rivers. Annually billions of gallons of water glide to the sea, brooks pass tiny hamlets, streams flow through towns, broad rivers cut cities in half. The bulk of this water reaches its salty destination unutilized, yet every inch each gallon of water falls is a possible source of electric current, which possesses the god-like qualities of heat, power and light.

This wasted flow of water and the whole problem of cheap electricity in the United States engaged the attention of President Roosevelt long before the people sent him to Washington as Chief Executive. Repeatedly he has emphasized the importance of a more thorough development of our water resources and a more widespread distribution of electric power. Through PWA, he has begun a double-barreled campaign to secure both for the Nation. He has encouraged gigantic projects to tap some of our hitherto wasted water energy and he has instituted expert surveys to determine exactly what are equitable electric rates with a view to developing plans for future utilization of additional available water power.

Acting under the Senate Joint Resolution of April 14, 1934, authorizing "necessary funds to conduct an investigation regarding rates charged for electrical energy and to prepare a report thereon," the President allocated $300,000 from PWA funds to the Federal Power Commission to make a rate survey. The first report made by the commission gives a graphic picture of rates paid for residential electric service in all cities of 50,000 or more. It covers 191 cities, comprising 49 per cent of all residential customers, urban and rural, in the United States. Later reports will include all communities of 1,000 or more population in each State.

Returns already received represent more than 97 per cent of the total sales to ultimate consumers by both privately owned and municipal electric utilities. The survey directs attention to the wide divergencies in the rates charged for electric service in communities similarly situated and possessing the same general characteristics.

This survey is the most comprehensive ever made in this country and forms a basis for any future inquiry into the habits and customs of our electric utilities. The first report presents a mere snapshot of the variety and complexity of rate schedules. Some extreme examples, however, illustrate the importance of such a study and the necessity for a more unified and equitable power program. For instance, one hamlet of twenty-seven persons reports eleven different rate schedules; one company serving fifty-eight thousand residential customers, bills them under five hundred and thirty different schedules.

The information was set forth in the form of typical bills for specified quantities of electricity, carefully chosen to cover the entire range of use for domestic purposes, from the small consumer whose use is limited to lighting, to the large consumer whose use approximates that required in what is popularly known as an "electrified home." Each company was requested to compute its bills in the light of these classifications and to submit its rate schedule so that the computations could be checked by the survey staff. Furnished with this information, it is believed that practically every interested consumer can compare his own monthly bill with those tabulated in the survey for his and other cities.

This valuable rate survey is only a part of the work which is being done by the Federal Power Commission. An additional $400,000 was allocated to it from PWA funds to prepare a "comprehensive program of public works for conservation, development, control and utilization of water power for the generation of electrical energy and its transmission and/or distribution to consumers; and, in furtherance of the preparation of such program, to investigate, collect and record data concerning the present cost of generation, transmission and distribution of electrical energy; the data concerning the control and utilization of the national water resources including location, capacity, development cost and relation to markets of power sites; also data concerning the relation of the hydro-electric industry to other industries and to interstate and foreign commerce." This report has not yet been made as the necessary investigation is still underway.

In addition to the fundamental studies which are being made by the Federal Power Commission by means of its PWA financing, a grant of $100,000 was made at the President's suggestion to the National Power Policy Committee. This committee was established for the "purpose of developing a plan for the closer coöperation of the several factors in electric power supply, both public and private, whereby national policy in power matters may be unified and electricity be made more broadly available at cheaper rates to industry, to domestic and particularly to agricultural consumers; the committee is to be advisory to the President." To this committee has been assigned the task of drawing together all the conclusions of the various commissions and experiments. "It is not to be merely a fact-finding body, but rather one for the development and unification of national power policy."

Moreover, practical experiments, such as the huge power projects inaugurated and supported by the President under the other branch of his program, will throw valuable additional light on the problem, which, in turn will be availed of by the National Power Policy Committee and the National Resources Board. Five hundred million dollars have already been allocated by PWA for definite projects to harness a portion of our potential water power. As we have seen, in the far Southwest, out of a deep canyon of the Colorado River, has arisen Boulder Dam; in the Northwest human ants are building the Grand Coulee and Bonneville dams on the Columbia River; in the valley of the Tennessee the war-time Wilson Dam has been brought into fuller use and the Norris and Wheeler dams are being rushed for completion in 1936.

Mammoth power plants, with intricate generators large enough to supply whole cities, are being erected beside the dams; land is being cleared for huge reservoirs, and thick transmission lines are being strung up to carry to home and factory the low-cost electricity that is to come.

This activity is only the beginning of a national plan to increase the supply of electric power and to bring down its cost. The desire to provide cheap electricity for the consumer has a social object since cheap electricity will raise, almost to a revolutionary extent, the standard of living in underprivileged homes. It will bring electric lights to families who have lived with lamps and candles; in homes where spring houses and cellars have provided dubious refrigeration it will protect food at proper temperatures; it will furnish heat for electric stoves and power for washing machines, sewing machines, lathes and pumps for the farmer and his wife; radios and electric fans will become possible farmhouse equipment as well as improved sanitary facilities, and, soon perhaps, television.

This is a pleasantly desirable prospect which, at best, will require a long time for its complete realization. But an experiment to demonstrate what can be accomplished with cheap electricity in less fortunate rural sections of the country is being conducted in the Tennessee Valley where 50 million dollars of PWA funds are being spent by an authority directed by Dr. Arthur E. Morgan, flood-control expert and former president of Antioch College; Dr. Harcourt A. Morgan, farm authority and for fifteen years president of the University of Tennessee, and David E. Lilienthal, lawyer and former member of the utilities commission of Wisconsin.

Two million persons live in the Tennessee Valley, a hammock-shaped section touching seven States which is the equivalent in size of about three-quarters of England. They are of old English stock, who have had their homes in this center of the historic southeastern section of the

United States from very early days. Airplanes pass over their heads; luxurious automobiles speed by them on highways; their very air gives passage to radio waves. Surrounded as they are by a more modern America, it is difficult to imagine that the introduction of electricity could be so dramatically incongruous to the mode of life of so many of them. Yet it is. More than once the TVA officials themselves have had startling evidence of this.

An example is the experience of an agent for the authority who opened an office in a small town to which transmission lines had just been extended. The inhabitants had apparently been eager to get electricity and the agent confidently prepared for a rush of business. But the first day passed without a customer appearing. Several similar days went by, and although the agent anxiously made it known that he was in town, still there were no customers. Finally, struck by an idea, he connected an electric bulb to the power lines and hung it in front of his office. Immediately there was a flood of applications. The agent had been a true psychologist. As one venerable citizen told him:

"I reckon none of us knowed light come through paltry wires like those 'til we seen it with our own eyes."

The history of the Tennessee Valley development dates back to the World War when Wilson Dam and two nitrate plants were erected at Muscle Shoals on the Tennessee River in Alabama. This national defense measure cost 150 million dollars, but after the war the plants became obsolete as the result of new processes, and the dam was allowed to stand idle. Senator George W. Norris of

Nebraska, over a period of years, persistently fought for a national use of this wasted power and even, on occasion, persuaded Congress to pass bills authorizing its development. Presidential vetoes (two by Coolidge and one by Hoover) balked his efforts. At the same time private interests were attempting to secure control of the properties, but these moves, including an offer of 5 million dollars from Henry Ford for a development that had cost the taxpayers thirty times that sum, were blocked in Congress by the public-spirited Nebraskan. Finally the sale to private power interests of a small portion of the power developed at Muscle Shoals was authorized, and the remainder of the electricity was allowed to go to waste.

When Mr. Roosevelt was elected President he evinced a keen interest in Muscle Shoals. With Senator Norris he made a tour of the Tennessee Valley, viewed Wilson Dam and the nitrate plants, and then returned to Washington. He had seen more in the valley than simply electrical power, for in a subsequent message to Congress he outlined a complete program of water, land and power development for the economic and social upbuilding of a great area. He said:

"It is clear that the Muscle Shoals development is but a small part of the potential public usefulness of the entire Tennessee River. Such use, if envisioned in its entirety, transcends mere power development; it enters the wide fields of flood control, soil erosion, afforestation, elimination from agricultural use of marginal lands, and distribution and diversification of industry. In short this power development of war days leads logically to national planning for a complete river watershed involving many states and the future lives and welfare of millions. It touches and gives life to all forms of human concerns."

This plan for social betterment is firmly grounded on the soil of good hard sense. It is almost as if the government said: We are going to harness the Tennessee and its tributaries by means of great dams and extract from its waters a gigantic supply of electric power. Then we shall distribute this power to as many people as possible at the least possible cost. Incidentally the cost here will serve as a yardstick by which to measure costs in other parts of the country. In this way we will raise the standard of living among the people of the valley as well as in neighboring communities.

To which this natural objection arises: How can you sell power to farmers who do not make enough money to buy it?

The answer is: We must find out why the farmers fail to make a living from their land, and apply a remedy.

Once the Tennessee Valley was a land of plenty. The pioneers who settled there found lush meadows for their cattle; fertile fields for corn and cotton and wheat; abundant forests which could be transformed into houses and cut for fire wood; fish and game for empty larders. But the thoughtless generations which followed them changed all this. The forests were ruthlessly destroyed and the water from rains and melting snow, with the natural coverage gone, rushed in torrents to the Tennessee, eating canyons and hollows in the sloping fields, carrying away valuable top soil and flooding homes. Persistent failure to rotate crops exhausted the fertility of the earth. At best, farming became a precarious occupation. Undernourished crops came to be completely dependent upon the whims of the weather and the now hostile river.

It is clear that such a situation must be changed if the farmer is to have any buying power at all. So TVA has engaged in a number of undertakings. It has begun reforestation projects; it is filling up gullies in fields and otherwise checking erosion; it is working out a program of flood control; it is distributing instruction on crop rotation and other farming problems. And all the while it is building its dams and power houses.

Altogether, it is expected that up to 300 million dollars will be spent in the Tennessee Valley in the course of the next six years, including power development and land renovation. PWA has approved loans and grants to cities which wish to build transmission and distributing systems so that they can make use of cheap TVA power. Ten million dollars have been earmarked for this purpose and one city, Knoxville, has been allotted $2,600,000 for the improvement and extension of its own system. Additional appeals for aid have been received from scores of towns and cities whose local governments are wistful for low-cost TVA power, but which are unable to raise enough money to build a distribution system or buy out the existing utility that continues to charge unduly high rates.

The unique accomplishments of TVA, while they cannot be fully listed until long after the whole project has been completed, are in the field of social betterment. These are startling, as some examples will show.

First there is the farmer who has obtained cheap electricity from TVA. A year ago, in his unpainted frame home, the man of a farm in the Tennessee Valley lived a life which can be compared only with that of a thirteenth-century serf. It is true he had no feudal lord to oppress him, but his standard of living was very little higher than his English ancestor of the Dark Ages. His wife, prematurely aged by excessive childbearing and hard work, cooked rude food over a smoking wood fire, washed in water brought in pails from a well, and sewed by lamp or candle light. The farmer himself chopped the wood for fuel, packed water for his stock and fed his horses and cattle in the dark on winter mornings. The children ruined their eyes studying by firelight. In common with a million others they all were anachronisms in modern America.

Now this farmer is able to have light in his home at the cost of a dozen eggs a week. For a few cents more an electric pump will bring tap water to his house and barn, and a heater will make it piping hot. He may have a radio—that much desired luxury-necessity, especially in the rural areas—and his wife an electric stove and a refrigerator. If he is a hill-farmer there is available to him and his craftsmen sons electric looms and lathes to turn out products which have a definite sales value in other parts of the country. If he lives in the lowlands the electricity will help him in the dairying which should become an important industry once floods are controlled in the grassy meadow bottoms.

To the city dweller likewise this cheap electric current means less labor, greater leisure and multiplied opportunities for self-culture. Obviously the most important advantage of TVA to him is the cheapness of the river-made electricity. But will it be cheap enough for the householder, already having trouble with his budget, to use it for all the gadgets he would like to have?

"Certainly," the TVA official answers, "and the more gadgets he has, the less expensive it will be."

This answer is in line with a theory that recently has been gaining adherents in the ranks of private power utility operators. It was stated concisely by one of the private operators, Samuel Ferguson, president of the Hartford Electric Light Company in Connecticut, when he said:

"A completely electrified home should be able to earn a rate of two cents or less for entire requirements of light, cooking, refrigeration, hot water, etc. This is an idea which has not as yet received universal acceptance, but in my opinion it must be done and done quickly. We find much more profit in the all-electric homes earning rates as low as 1.7 cents per kilowatt hour than we do in the average home at four and a half cents or the small user at eight cents, and certainly the users are more pleased."

The factual answer to the question whether or not the householder can afford a greater use of electricity, if charged lower rates, is given in Tupelo, Mississippi, one of the thirteen municipalities which have signed contracts with the Authority. There the bills for electricity have been cut nearly in half since TVA replaced the private company. The average home in this town, using electricity for lighting, radio, refrigeration, vacuum cleaning and perhaps washing, now pays about $2 a month. The completely electric home, using power for cooking and heating water, costs a dollar more each month. And these rates are likely to be even lower when the whole system goes into operation.

These facts are difficult for the privately owned company to explain to the customer who ruefully compares his monthly bill for light alone with what his more fortunate fellow citizen in the Tennessee Valley pays for both light and power for diversified purposes.

But TVA has done one more thing to show that cheap electricity has indirect, as well as direct benefits. It has built the town of Norris.

In the heart of the Clinch River district, a region dotted with the rude shacks and dilapidated frame houses of the native farmer, lies this town in a cluster of pine and magnolia trees. It does not look like any other rural town in the whole country; it more closely resembles a fine suburban small home development. Each house has been designed by a competent architect. Each has a big yard, and in many cases two to five acres of ground spread around it for gardening purposes. There are shower baths, cedar cabinets, sleeping porches and model kitchens, and each house is lighted, heated and air-conditioned with electricity. Moreover, the same force that does these things is there to polish the woodwork, clean the rugs, wash the dishes, do the ironing and dispose of the garbage. The average rent for one of these houses is twenty-two dollars a month.

Where, in the entire world, can a man and his family live as comfortably for so little?

Granted that a case has been made out for cheap TVA power it might well be asked where the average householder is going to get the money with which to buy expensive electrical equipment for his home. The TVA officials have answered that, too. They have made it possible for the home owner to purchase refrigerators and electric stoves and water pumps on monthly installments at a price 30 per cent below the price that the cash buyer pays in the rest of the country. The credit for this additional advantage accruing to those fortunates who live in this region of low-cost electricity goes to the Electric Home and Farm Authority, a favored foster child of TVA. This organization, which has a capital of one million dollars and additional credit up to 10 millions with the Reconstruction Finance Corporation, has persuaded leading electrical equipment manufacturers to make available simpler, and sometimes smaller, but always less expensive units, to the valley people. This equipment is sold to the householder by the regular dealer who gets his money from the EHFA. Then the householder pays back the money to EHFA over a period of months, or even years. Some of these appliances have now been placed on the national market by the manufacturers, but for the time being EHFA financing is confined to the low-power-rate areas in the Tennessee Valley.

This is the picture in broad outline of TVA at the present time. Soon, it is to be expected, the idea will be extended to other sections of the country. Moreover, TVA—and this is one of the main reasons for its establishment—will provide a "yardstick" for the measurement of similar rates in other parts of the Nation, with the result of forcing pretty generally a reduction of private utility charges. And while doing this, TVA itself, under efficient management, will return to the taxpayers, with both a money and a social profit, the capital invested in this enterprise.

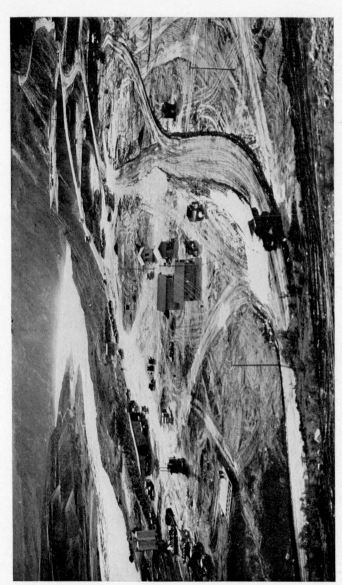

Excavating the west bank of the Columbia River for the Grand Coulee dam and power project being constructed by the Bureau of Reclamation with an allotment of $15,000,000 from the Public Works Administration. This project will cost about $63,000,000 and will produce 2,200,000,000 kilowatt-hours of firm energy; 42,300 man-months of direct employment will be provided.

This TVA enterprise has appealed particularly to the public imagination because of its magnitude and on account of the broad social concept that underlies it. Yet this is not the only front upon which the government, under its PWA program, has been advancing against those utility interests that have been exacting unconscionable tribute from the people of the United States for so many years.

In Wyoming preliminary work already has been started for the building of the Casper-Alcova Dam, another power and reclamation project undertaken in the hope that the land brought under cultivation will be capable of producing enough alfalfa hay to carry through the hard winters the great herds of cattle that now periodically, for want of forage, have to be driven to the far-off Texas Panhandle to be wintered. In Nebraska, the Sutherland project will produce power in return for PWA dollars while in the far northeast corner of Maine a study is being made of the plan to harness the mighty tides in Passamaquoddy Bay to provide light and power for the New England States.

In addition to financing these and other great regional power projects, PWA has approved applications for loans and grants involving rural electrification. One of these, an allotment of $575,000, was made to the Southeastern Nebraska Public Power District for the installation of an electric distribution system to serve approximately 1,400 customers.

The security taken for this loan is revenue bonds with mortgage provisions, to be repaid serially by 1955. Two important conditions were made to this allotment. The first was for the protection of the taxpayers' money loaned through PWA. It required that the applicant should agree always to maintain rates sufficient to cover debt service on the loan and provide a reasonable surplus. The second condition was for the protection of the consumers of the electric current. It provides that the applicant shall purchase power under a contract satisfactory to the Administrator, which contract, however, shall not require the district to pay, during the loan period, a rate higher than three cents per kilowatt hour for current delivered at the consumer's meter, up to 50,000 KWH, or two cents per kilowatt hour for current in excess of this amount.

It has been the policy of PWA to make loans for municipal power plants when such projects are sound from a legal, economic and engineering point of view. The question of public policy involved is left to the municipality concerned. However, we have applied certain general rules. We have decided not to approve a project unless it is self-liquidating at rates lower than or approximately equal to those of the utility company serving the community, and we have determined that the earnings of the proposed system must be applied to the system itself wherever possible under the State law and not siphoned into the general tax fund except in amounts not greater than the taxes which would be paid in case the system were privately owned. Where the existing private system has transmission lines or plant equipment that can be merged into the proposed municipal enterprise, we have encouraged its purchase at a reasonable figure. Finally, we have always given the private utility an opportunity to meet the city's proposed rates, and, if this is done, the city is afforded a second chance to lower still further its anticipated charges. But we have uniformly reserved the right to help a city which desires its own power plant even if the suggested rates will not be lower than those of the private utility.

It has been my position that there are definite intangible values flowing to a community that owns and operates its own utilities. A strong case can be made for the proposition that if the people of a community want to own their own public utilities and are able to finance them, they should not be denied that opportunity merely because the rates necessary to be charged in order to pay overhead and to liquidate are equal to or perhaps even slightly in excess of rates already currently charged by privately owned utilities. We do not attempt to dictate to another what he may buy within his means even if we regard him as being extravagant. In addition to which, there is a considerable price which a municipality can afford to pay in order to rid itself of the domineering tactics and the corrupting influences too often resorted to in the past by private utility interests.

In many cities, and even in a number of States, the utilities have long dominated public affairs in their own interest in two ways—first, by a judicious, if surreptitious, selection and support of hand-picked candidates for legislative, executive and judicial offices, who can be counted upon if elected, never to fail readily to recognize their masters' voices; and, second, by a corrupt use of money at the polls and in city councils and State legislatures where sinister favors are also frequently available to supplement the use of money. To add insult to injury, these "operating expenses" have to be paid in the end by the betrayed utility users with a generous margin added for good measure.

Having shaken off, as the result of a persistent fight carried on for more than a generation, the throttling hand of the railroads upon their affairs, the people have once more found it necessary to rally to the standard in the never-ending war to preserve the integrity of their own institutions. This time they are in a hand to hand struggle with the utility interests.

In one respect, the utility overlords, while more arrogant even than "People-be-damned" Vanderbilt and his crowd, have been more subtle. They had taken a page from the record of the failure of the railroads to continue to dominate the political thought of the people of the United States. Instead of holding the stock of the privately owned utilities closely, they adopted the policy of so-called customer ownership after ingeniously devising a method to maintain control by printing for themselves a few certificates of a special kind of stock. It became as much the function of a power company to sell its own stock by high-pressure methods as it was to market electric current. Whether or not this bright thought emanated from the teeming brain of Samuel Insull, under the genius of his leadership it developed into a perfect flower. It was thought that with thousands upon thousands of stockholders permeating the mass of the people, a public assault even upon a notoriously corrupt utility might easily be repulsed.

Unfortunately for these clever manipulators, the stock market crash of 1929 exposed the flank that the utility interests thought was carefully protected by serried ranks of customer stockholders. Duped investors found, in many instances, that they had been buying "securities" of the substance of not even pure water. Already users of electric current had begun to agitate for an overdue reduction in rates or for publicly owned plants. When they were joined by an army of disillusioned stockholders who had painfully discovered that all they had to show for their life savings were nicely engraved certificates in some holding company that possessed no tangible property or franchises; that operated no plant and merely disported itself as a financial merman in the irridescent spray thrown up on the golden-sanded beach of an economic empire that existed only in the imagination, then indeed were they eager to strike out against those who had tricked and deceived them into paying huge sums to be used to undermine popular government.

Private utility operators who are having a difficult time these days, have only themselves to blame. History to them is written in a dead language. Greedily selfish, they lack intelligence. For so many years had they ruled with an iron hand, squeezing the last cent of profit out of the consumer, that they had come to believe that their financial and political power could never be checked.

With the example of Samuel Insull before them, it is not to be wondered at that many people have decided that they are willing to pay some price for the privilege of protecting their institutions from further undermining by the private utility interests. And if the people can protect themselves from corrupting and subversive influences and at the same time supply themselves with power at rates equal to or lower than those charged by private utilities, what reasonable argument is there against the right of the public to own and operate their utilities?

Yet as might be expected, there has been bitter opposition to our acting favorably on requests for funds to build municipal utility systems. Subterranean influence has been brought to bear and every sort of legal obstacle has been thrown in the way of such loans. The private utilities, by direct frontal or by flank attacks, have held up many projects month after month.

Typical of the resistance put up by the private companies to public ownership of utilities is the somewhat long but illuminating story of the Greenwood County project at Buzzard's Roost, South Carolina. This point, on the Saluda River, was recommended as a possible power site after the army's survey of the Nation's streams, and the people of the county decided that they wanted to make and distribute their own current.

The local power company concerned is the Southern Public Utilities Company, a subsidiary of the Duke Power system. The city of Greenwood, largest in the county, owns its own distribution system and purchases electricity from the Southern. The rural districts are without electricity and many of the local textile companies obtain their power from their own steam plants. Only 21 per cent of the total power proposed to be sold, according to the application from the county, was being furnished by the private utility.

When the application for a loan and grant of $2,767,000 to the county, secured by revenue bonds payable from gross revenues and additionally secured by a statutory mortgage on the property, reached PWA in Washington, it was accompanied by letters from political leaders in the State urging its acceptance. Senators Byrnes and Smith pointed out the value it would have for the community, as did Congressman McSwain who wrote:

"The project for Greenwood County affords one of the very best illustrations of the wisdom and advisability of the PWA. The unemployed from five surrounding counties were listed by the Federal authorities at 14,000 and, as soon as the money is made available for the above project, 1,200 of these can be immediately put to work in clearing the basin and in all preliminary work, and then the number of employed will be increased from time to time and employment will also be given in building the rural electrification lines, and there is prospect of additional and small industries and business projects developing in view of the cheap power to be offered.

"Furthermore, to show that the short period of time for the repayment of the loan by PWA is not based upon high rates, the fact is that the rates proposed by the Greenwood municipal project are actually slightly lower than the rates offered by TVA."

In June of 1934 the project was approved by the three examining divisions of PWA and a resolution prepared for presentation to the Special Board. Suddenly the Duke Endowment began a noisy protest, asserting, in effect, that the modest Greenwood County project would bring starvation and ruin to the hospitals, schools, orphanages and churches supported in part by it in both South and North Carolina.

This devastating picture of impending doom, so vividly painted in the protest, caused PWA to send the project to the Electric Power Board of Review for a thorough study. There it was discovered that the Duke Endowment, the Doris Duke Trust and the Duke Power Company, all creations of the late James B. Duke, the tobacco magnate, were so inextricably tied together that only a lawyer of unusual ability could unravel the legal skein into which they have been skillfully intertwined. On the surface it appeared that only the finer humanitarianism of the Duke-ites was pained by the prospect of lower rates to the people. Nothing was said about the business of the Duke Power Company in Greenwood County; it was the benevolent Duke Endowment that would suffer irreparable damage unless consumers paid more for electricity than it was worth.

A letter came to me from George G. Allen, who was careful to explain that he was writing in his capacity as chairman of the Duke Foundation, not as president of the Duke Power Company, which office he also (and presumably incidentally) held. He concluded his protest with this disingenuous threat:

"I shall be under the necessity of making known to all the beneficiaries of the endowment the action your committee has taken and its likely consequences, in order that the people of the Carolinas may understand if this great philanthropy by Mr. Duke should fail them that the failure has been caused through unfair competition, a use of the taxes the Duke Power Company and other concerns are paying to put such concerns out of business."

The Jekyll-Hydeian rôle of Mr. Allen and the effective scrambling of the Duke Endowment, the Doris Duke Trust and the Duke Power Company have led to so much confusion that people often refer to the Duke Power Company as though it were purely and simply an elee-mosynary institution. Yet an examination of the set-up of the three shows that a relatively small amount of the power profits goes to charity. As of December 31, 1933, the Duke Power Company had outstanding the following common stock:

> 122,647 shares owned by the Duke Endowment;
> 127,904 shares owned by the Doris Duke Trust;
> 759,498 shares owned by the others.
>
> ———————
>
> 1,010,049 shares outstanding.

On this stock in 1933 dividends were paid totaling $4,040,192 as follows:

> $490,588 to the Duke Endowment;
> $511,616 to the Doris Duke Trust;
> $3,037,988 to others.

The Duke Power Company was certainly letting its right hand know what its left hand was doing. It was making a practical application of the old adage that "Charity covers a multitude of sins." Not only was it hiding behind the flimsy skirts of its own philanthropy, it was also raising a tremendous fuss over what would have been a loss of business of not to exceed one-third of one per cent if the Greenwood County project should go into operation. The fact is that it was proposed to dis-tribute more than 80 per cent of the power to be devel-oped at Buzzard's Roost to new industrial and rural cus-tomers at a reasonable rate, something the Duke Power Company does not seem to be able to do.

A hearing was held by the Electric Power Board of Review in July of 1934 with officials of the company present to make their statements. Engineers claimed that the cost of the project had been underestimated and lawyers argued that the project was designed to give one particular textile mill the benefit of most of the industrial current to be generated. It was urged that to supply current to cotton mills in the Greenwood area at a price less than that fixed by the Duke Power Company would result in an unfair advantage to those mills.

A vice-president of the Duke Power Company repeated Mr. Allen's charge of unfairness. And, as might have been expected, officials of institutions receiving financial aid from the Duke Endowment, protested any action which might reduce the incomes of their institutions. If they sensed the injustice of levying enormous tribute upon the people in order that their own favored institutions might receive gratuities, they gave no evidence of it. Thus, as often is the case, a fine social enterprise was made to serve as a handmaiden to an anti-social purpose.

The reviewing board, in passing on the objections, decided that $85,000 additional should be allotted for construction of the project. The Greenwood County authorities agreed to modify the plan to have one mill consume a preponderance of the power and listed several municipalities and mills as additional potential customers. In reply to the claim of unfair competition, based on the fact that a publicly owned utility is tax exempt, the board stated that the State of South Carolina and the United States, through their representatives, "have determined that municipal electric-light projects shall not be taxed and that corporations for profit engaged in the sale of electricity shall be taxed. The National Industrial Recovery Act (Title II, Sections 202 and 203) authorized the administrator to finance such projects as that of Greenwood County and does not limit him to enterprises not in competition with existing corporations for profit. Hence, it does not appear that taxation is a factor to be considered by the Electric Power Board of Review.

"Further, in response to a complaint that the establishment of a municipal utility to sell current at a price less than that offered by a private utility is inconsistent with the policy of Title I of the National Industrial Recovery Act," the board went on to say, "experience shows that a reduction of rates results in the increase of the current sold and in the long run may result in increase of revenue. This is proved by the experience of the Tennessee Valley with Tupelo, Mississippi, that of the Potomac Electric Power Company in the City of Washington, that of the Ontario Hydro-electric Commission and a number of municipally and privately operated enterprises throughout the United States."

Following the decision of the Electric Power Board of Review, the project—now requiring an allotment of $2,852,000—was approved and the Greenwood County authorities were so notified. But there were still two legal impediments to be overcome. One of them was the question whether or not the county could build a power system under the laws of South Carolina. There was no precedent for such a project being financed by the issuance of revenue bonds and there was a possibility that the courts would not be favorable if the cost should be charged against the general revenues. PWA asked the county to hold up construction until the State supreme court could rule on the matter. As the result of a test suit, the county was given the right by the court to go ahead with the project.

Although this suit gave it its day in court, the Duke Power Company was not satisfied; it wanted two days. After trying in vain to persuade the State courts to delay the project, the Duke interests asked the Federal courts for an injunction. They challenged the constitutionality of the National Industrial Recovery Act and charged that the money allocated by PWA was insufficient to build the dam and pay for the necessary power equipment. The courts have not yet decided this question.

. . . . . .

By January of 1935, twelve municipal power projects had been completed. Forty-eight others were under construction; thirty-four more had been approved by the power board, and about seventy-one were under consideration. The total amount allotted at that time for this purpose was $48,784,300.

One of the most important accomplishments of PWA, although an indirect one, has been a saving to consumers of millions of dollars through the lowering of rates by the private utilities to meet the charges proposed by applicants for public power projects. The rejection or withdrawal of some of the 200 applications that PWA did not approve was the result of this reduction of rates by the private companies to a point where there seemed no necessity or justification for a municipal plant.

These "yardsticks" provided by both municipal and Federal enterprises are so valuable that they alone would warrant PWA's expenditures for power undertakings. The municipal projects have caused private utilities to adjust their rates downward in wide areas and the Federal projects have brought about rate adjustments over still larger expanses of territory.

But more significant than the "yardstick" quality of these Federal and municipal power projects is the fact that their development marks the beginning of an age of electricity for the United States—an age which will make the mid-Victorian marvels of steam and gas seem primitive and crude. Once the tremendous locked-up reserve of electrical power in the streams and rivers and coal mines of the country has been adequately employed; once electricity as cheap as water, if not as free as air, is available to every householder; once equipment to utilize more generally the coming low-cost power has been perfected by the inventive genius of America, a magical and hitherto unimagined civilization will have dawned in the Western World.

Chapter VII

MODERNIZING TRANSPORT

THE traveler is an important figure in the social and commercial life of a country. To business he is as necessary as factories or shops. He is an instrumentality in the more general distribution of commercial products and in the establishment of the commercial credit that makes that distribution possible. Socially he is an important factor in the destruction of sectional barriers. He begets friendships wherever he goes and he brings home with him from each trip an increased toleration for other customs and communities. If, here in America, he had been as numerous and as mobile a hundred years ago as he is now there might have been no Civil War.

Upon his peregrinations depends an impressive percentage of the American people, both for commerce and for pleasure.

Long ago the Federal Government recognized the consequence of the traveler. It has built roads and harbors for him and his goods and protected him and them with armed authority on sea and land. It has provided a Coast Guard Service to rescue him when he is in trouble at sea; it has given valuable rights-of-way to railroad companies which wished to serve him. More recently it has aided his progress through the sky by the erection of beacons for airplanes and the building of airports.

Thus, when PWA was created, the traveler was one of the first to receive some of the benefits arising from the distribution of its funds. The expenditure of the approximately 600 million dollars on roads, described in another chapter, was of great aid to the automobile traveler, whether he journeyed for pleasure or for commerce.

A second mode of travel helped by PWA money is the railroad. Of course, I do not intend to make the traveler solely responsible for the loans of approximately 200 million dollars to railroads because there were at least two other outstanding reasons for such an allocation of funds, but the railroads' vital importance to the traveler and his to the Nation were certainly underlying causes for this expenditure.

The surface reasons for these loans were both patent and appealing. PWA had been evoked to prime the pump of business. One of the best ways of doing this was to spend money through the railroads, where a large proportion of each dollar goes for labor, with another substantial percentage for material from the heavy industries, in which unemployment has been most acute.

The railroads, in good years one of the Nation's biggest spenders, had been forced to cut down their costs to such a degree during the depression that many of them had abandoned earlier plans for extensions and modernization of their equipment. They were operating with skeleton crews; in some cases with less than half their regular personnel. Aid was needed to put these employees back to work.

How well these particular loans worked to create employment may be judged from a summary of the reports made by the railroads at the end of the first year of PWA help. Our money had created approximately 65 million man-hours of employment, extending into every State, and was responsible for the reëmployment of 90,000 railroad employees.

In addition, about 150,000 persons in other industries were put to work supplying the materials purchased by the railroads at a cost of about 100 million dollars.

Besides these benefits of increased work resulting from the railroad loans, this money has enabled the railroad companies to make badly needed and long deferred improvements to their properties. From these the public has benefited in improved service and greater safety. Much modern equipment, including streamlined trains and air-conditioned passenger coaches, has been purchased. Many old and unsafe wooden cars have been replaced with safer steel coaches. New rails have been laid. Bridges and tunnels have been repaired or replaced with more modern and stronger structures capable of carrying the heavy traffic of to-day.

Probably the most striking railroad loan was that of $80,650,000 to the Pennsylvania Railroad of which 60 million dollars was for the completion of the electrification of its line between Washington and New York City. This has been the largest single loan made to a private concern by PWA; it was the first of the railroad loans and it supplied funds for the largest private construction job carried out anywhere in the world in 1934.

A prophetic picture of the growth of cities in the

United States by 1950 was given to railroad men by the Pennsylvania when it announced its electrification project in 1928. By 1950, said the railroad officials, the metropolitan area of New York City would extend thirty miles or more into New Jersey and a similar distance into Long Island, and the population of the area would be close to 30 million persons. Moreover, before many more years, they added, there would be a practically unbroken line of communities from the Hudson River to the Potomac.

It is obvious that the heavy steam locomotive of the past, with its relatively slow acceleration, its noise and its smoke, is not suited to such an urban area as that pictured by the Pennsylvania. There is an increasing need for a faster, neater, and quieter type of locomotive as population becomes more dense.

In the electric locomotive the Pennsylvania saw a way to meet the changes which the phenomenal growth of cities was requiring of the railroads. The electric train would be faster because of its quickness in starting and stopping and cheaper because its speed would make possible a greater utilization of the right-of-way. It would be a great gain all around if there would be no further necessity for the clumsy encumbrances of the steam line—the water tanks, the coal yards, the ash pits, the turntables and the roundhouses—which have no place in the modern city. Moreover, the electric train would be ideal for short-haul passenger runs with commuters from suburban areas to the business districts of the larger towns, and the electric freight train, swifter than steam, would fill a vital need by bringing from the South and West fruits and vegetables of the freshness demanded by the great city markets.

For nearly four years work on the electrification of the line between New York and the Capital was carried on by the Pennsylvania. Money for the construction of the overhead wire system, the great transformers, the cars and locomotives was obtained through the usual channels of financing and from the railroad company's treasury, but in 1933, due to the depression, funds were no longer obtainable. New financing, usually a normal investment process, was brought to a standstill everywhere in the country.

Colonel Waite, once railroads had been selected as one of the better ways by which men could be put to work, recalled this suspended work on the Pennsylvania Railroad with whose electrification program he was familiar. He made a special trip to the Pennsylvania's headquarters in Philadelphia and spent considerable time discussing the advantages of continuing the electrification with government funds at a time when so many people needed work. However, after he had convinced the railroad officials that they ought to borrow some 80 million dollars from PWA, a difficulty arose. General W. W. Atterbury, president of the railroad, was unwilling to give security, as required by the Act. Finally Frank C. Wright, who had accepted the post of chief of PWA's division of transportation loans, persuaded the Pennsylvania to change its mind. Immediately the work of rushing the application through the examining groups was begun.

In addition to the customary examinations by the financial and legal staffs the application was referred to the Interstate Commerce Commission in accordance with the provision of the Act. It was also submitted to Joseph B.

Eastman, Federal coördinator of railroads. These two approvals having been obtained, the contract was signed on New Year's Eve, 1934. The loan to the railroad comprised 37 million dollars for electrification; 23 millions for 100 new electric locomotives; 17 millions for 7,000 new freight cars and $3,650,000 for 100,000 tons of new rails.

Immediate employment to thousands of workers was given by the railroad in February, 1934, when construction began again. About 15,000 Pennsylvania employees were called back to work and, directly and indirectly, a total of 25,000 workers were given jobs for the year. Six States and the District of Columbia had men on the company's payroll, and about thirty-six States benefited indirectly through the purchase of materials. In many places companies whose shops and factories had been practically idle were compelled to operate on double shifts to fill the railroad's orders, which had amounted to 41 million dollars at the end of the year.

Just as there were impressive employment benefits from this loan, so were there satisfactions to the public in the better service the railroad was able to give. The new electric equipment covered 364 miles of line and 1,405 miles of track when the Washington to New York service was opened on January 28, 1935. With this the railroad was able to cut forty-five minutes from its running time between the two cities, a saving of approximately 20 per cent.

On the sea, another medium for the traveler, PWA also has expended sizeable sums. The navy, which serves the double purpose of protecting our foreign commerce and the homeland, received an outright grant of 238 million dollars for its shipbuilding program. The money received by the navy was allocated for the following ships: 2 aircraft carriers, 1 heavy cruiser, 3 light cruisers, 4 submarines, 2 gunboats and 20 destroyers, a total of 32 ships. Part of the building program was awarded to navy yards; part to private shipbuilders. The primary purpose of the grant, as with all PWA allocations, was to relieve unemployment. So each contract for the construction of a vessel awarded to private industry contained a provision requiring speedy execution of the work. It read:

"Owing to the national emergency existing making it imperative that the maximum number of men be returned to gainful employment without delay, and to effectuate the purpose of the NIRA approved June 16, 1933, the contractor hereby expressly agrees that from the beginning he will prosecute the work with the utmost vigor and dispatch and will make every possible effort, without reference to the otherwise normal rate of progress, to accomplish the maximum amount of work within the first and second years thereof."

In addition, the Secretary of the Navy requested the builders to order all materials at the earliest possible date, even though much of them might not be needed until later. In this way industries directly and indirectly connected with shipbuilding were assured of immediate work.

Because the ships to be constructed, with the exception of one cruiser, were of a new type and design, it was necessary to prepare special plans for all of them. This involved a great amount of design work, so much so that ordinarily the program would have been delayed a year or more, but the Navy Department continued to coöperate with PWA by rushing this phase of the work. A provision was made in the shipbuilding code permitting employees engaged in designing, engineering and ordering materials to work up to forty-eight hours a week, and all available draftsmen and designers were put to work under this exception.

The design staff of the Bureau of Construction and Repair of the Navy Department was organized in such a manner that subsections of it, acting as a "traveling design staff," were sent from yard to yard to go over plans and specifications. Wherever possible they gave approvals on the spot, thus eliminating many delays which would have occurred if everything had had to go through the usual central clearing office.

Naval statisticians have estimated that the cost of materials purchased by the shipbuilder from sources outside his plant is about 40 per cent of the value of the contract, so that in prosecuting the PWA program the navy will have made purchases amounting to about 100 million dollars.

A breakdown of the dollar spent on a naval vessel shows that about 84 per cent of it is paid directly to labor. About 40 per cent goes to the men working on the ship and the other 44 per cent to labor away from the yards. The materials used in constructing the vessel come from every State in the Union, although the heaviest purchase is of steel. The total bill for steel in the PWA-Navy program was $28,560,000.

Besides the money spent for ships to protect our land from possible human enemies, PWA presented approx-

imately 25 million dollars to another seafaring service
whose fine and humane job is to protect the traveler at sea
from his cosmic enemies—storms, unusual tides, fogs,
floating wrecks and icebergs. This service is the United
States Coast Guard, which, in 1934 alone, rendered valuable assistance to ships in trouble on the two oceans, the
Great Lakes and the Gulf of Mexico, saving many lives
and preserving cargoes and other property valued at more
than 40 million dollars.

With its public works allotments, the Coast Guard by
February 1, 1935, had completed building, and had assigned to duty, five 165-foot cutters, nine 165-foot patrol
boats, four 110-foot harbor tugs and ten new amphibian
planes. In addition, some of the money has been used for
repairs on other boats, on Coast Guard stations and
boathouses.

The new cutters are the first Coast Guard boats built
especially for heavy ice-breaking. Their seven-eighth-
inch steel hulls are capable of breaking through solid ice
two feet thick, and they are able to venture out to sea
in any weather. Within three months of their being com-
missioned they saved four ships in distress because of
winter storms.

The new amphibians have been assigned to various
Coast Guard air stations for use in assistance, rescue and
patrol work. They are of particular value for sighting
ships in distress, thus enabling the rescue boats to reach
the scene of the disaster without losing valuable time in
searching. Some of the planes are equipped for ambulance
service, and all have ample space in which to carry food
and medical supplies to ice-bound ships or isolated com-

PWA aids transport on land and sea.

munities in distress. One of the new planes holds the world's record for amphibians, 191 miles an hour, and all of them have a cruising speed of 167 miles an hour.

PWA funds are being used also by the Coast Guard to build seven 328-foot cutters, the largest vessels ever employed in the service. They are now being completed in the navy yards at Philadelphia, Brooklyn and Charleston. These will be equipped to carry one amphibian on their decks and they will be used for shore assistance work, derelict destruction, ice patrol service along the American-European route in the North Atlantic, and for special jobs in other waters. One of the boats, at least, will be assigned to Alaskan duty. There it will act as a traveling hospital for remote settlements, supplying the inhabitants with medical and dental aid. Besides, it will protect the seal herds from poaching, and enforce the fishing laws.

Finally, in this summary of PWA's assistance to the traveler, there is the latest medium of transportation—the air. Destined to become the most important of all the trio of land, sea and air for the traveler-in-a-hurry, this medium has not been neglected. Up to February of 1935, allotments of slightly more than 3 million dollars had been made to the Bureau of Air Commerce for the establishment and improvement of lighted airways, the construction of landing fields, the installation of radio equipment and for general experimental work.

As the volume of traffic by air increases, the necessity for well-lighted airways to protect airplanes with their cargoes of human lives and valuable mail becomes ever greater. In the last few years, as the result of improved airplanes, night flying has become common, and the majority of air travelers have grown accustomed to the reassuring sight of the beacon lights which outline the course.

More lighted airways are still needed, however, so a good part of the grant to the Bureau of Air Commerce has gone for beacon lights. More than half a million dollars was allocated for a new airway from St. Paul, Minnesota, to the Pacific Coast through the Northwest, and almost as much was granted for an airway between Washington, D. C., and Nashville, Tennessee. Many other and shorter routes were also constructed with PWA funds.

Another important assistance rendered the Bureau of Air Commerce has been the financing of a "master series" of aviation navigation maps covering the entire country. Including as it does the geographical characteristics of the land, population centers, political boundaries and significant features such as beacon lights, airports and radio stations, this cartographical project has been described by Rex Martin, assistant director of Air Commerce, as "the first comprehensive detailed map of the United States ever published." To complete the eighty-seven small maps which will make up the entire chart would have taken about ten years with only the bureau's usual funds to depend upon. With PWA's help they will be finished by the end of 1935.

In addition to this work about 2,000 aircraft landing fields were built by CWA labor with funds supplied from the PWA appropriation. Municipalities were encouraged to provide the land and the Air Bureau supervised the actual construction. In January of 1934, as these types of projects got under way, more than 51,000 men were employed in forty-one States.

Both the army and navy air forces also have been aided by PWA, each having been given $7,500,000. The money was used to buy new airplanes and to modernize equipment rapidly becoming obsolete. In the navy 168 new planes were purchased from eleven sources in seven States. They included combat, bombing, training and experimental types of the latest designs. The army's purchases included a group of sixty-four huge Martin bombers with a speed of more than 200 miles an hour and thirty low-wing attack planes whose three-blade propellers will give them an even greater speed.

Chapter VIII

PUBLIC HEALTH

On a grassy knoll in Washington, overlooking the Potomac River, is a cluster of buildings little known to the residents of the city and completely ignored by the tourist. Yet behind their walls a grim war against disease is being waged, the story of which is as dramatic as that of any of the political struggles in the Nation's Capital. World leaders in science know the structures, and millions of Americans unwittingly owe their health and lives to the workers who do research there. These buildings are the home of the National Institute of Health, maintained by the government through the Public Health Service.

In the Institute's laboratories are handled each day matters that vitally concern the health of every adult and child in the country. Even in the now so commonplace an occurrence as the inoculation of a child against diphtheria by a family doctor, the Institute plays an important rôle. The purity of the antitoxin used must have been approved by the Institute's scientists, and the Public Health Service must have inspected and certified the laboratory and methods of the manufacturer before he is given a Treasury Department license to sell his product.

When strange diseases appear in cities, or rural districts, the health commissioner of the State affected appeals at once to the Public Health Service for aid. A plea may come in this form: "There's a new disease out here. Many of our people are sick. Won't you come and help us prevent its spread?"

A research worker packs his bag and races out to the afflicted area. Perhaps he is able to diagnose the trouble in a short time, but in some cases an appeal such as the one I have mentioned may start researches that will take years to complete. Never, however, does the Institute give up until some way of checking the disease has been found. Some of its most famed victories have been won from such formidable opponents as spotted fever, Parrot fever, typhus, pellagra and deer-fly fever.

These and other valuable services were performed by the Public Health Service long before PWA was established to provide employment on socially desirable projects. In addition to its coöperation with State and local authorities in public health matters and its investigation of disease and supervision of vaccines, serums, toxins and other biological products, the Service has maintained quarantine stations and marine hospitals; supervised the medical examination of aliens and prospective immigrants and provided medical service in Federal prisons. But, important as it is, its work has been handicapped by a lack of funds.

Despite many achievements in the field of medicine and in disease prevention and a greatly increased knowledge of environmental factors which affect health, this Nation so far has failed to develop a comprehensive program for the preservation of public health. In the past it has required an unusually striking condition, such as a wide-

spread epidemic, to provide the stimulation to arouse public interest to demand real progress. Without minimizing
the great advances made by the medical profession, the
truth is the American people are not so healthy as they
might be. Evidence demonstrates that much suffering
might be avoided by the more general and efficient application of that scientific knowledge with which we are
already amply supplied.

The general idea of society's responsibilities for public
health has been too narrow. We are coming to see that,
in addition to watching over such things as sanitation,
pure water and foods and the control of infectious diseases, the State should assist in cutting down infant and
mother mortality, in the spreading of knowledge of personal hygiene and in the care of persons suffering from
the more serious diseases. It is fundamental that the full
safeguarding of the public health requires that all members of society have decent housing, proper living standards and adequate medical care.

To help the Public Health Service amplify its work,
PWA allotted $8,119,479 for quarantine vessels and sta-
tions, medical research, marine hospitals, border inspection stations and plague laboratories. A part of the money
was used to organize and supervise about 29 million
dollars worth of work done by CWA and FERA workers
on sanitary privy construction and in malaria swamp
elimination.

One of the major health safeguards of the country is
the quarantine service. Its alert force protects the Nation
from such dangerous diseases as cholera, bubonic plague,
yellow fever, typhus, leprosy and smallpox, all of which

are prevalent in the Orient, Africa and South America—places touched every day by ships or airplanes en route to America. The possibility of bubonic plague or typhus sweeping the United States may seem ridiculous to younger generations accustomed to comparative security from epidemics, but not so long ago, before the time of the quarantine service, calamities of this nature were frequent. In 1850 cholera along the Mississippi River swept away nearly 60,000 persons in a few months. A harrowing account of the voyage of a cholera ship laden with plague-stricken immigrants up the Mississippi was written by Mark Twain, and other and earlier authors have dwelt upon the terror and horror that have accompanied similar murrains.

The quarantine service always has been handicapped in its work by poor floating equipment. Before 1918 it operated with second-hand yachts and after the war it fell heir to some boats not wanted by the navy and army. In fifteen years these ships, none too good at first, became utterly obsolete. In addition to the trouble the quarantine workers themselves experienced, there were complaints from merchant vessels. The slow, inadequate quarantine ships caused delays, and these were quite costly, particularly to the larger boats with perishable cargoes.

PWA funds enabled the Service to build from blueprints supplied by its own architect fifteen modern boats, equipped with disinfecting apparatus, small laboratories and ambulance facilities. The hulls are of wrought iron which is believed to be superior in corrosion resistance and of greater longevity than steel, and the latest Diesel engines have been installed. The boats have improved materially the quarantine service at the ports to which they have been assigned.

Another notable activity of the Public Health Service is the maintenance of marine hospitals for the care of sailors and workers connected with the sea. Slightly more than 4 million dollars of the money given by PWA to the Service have been used to construct new hospitals and improve existing ones. The largest of the new hospitals is one being built in New York at an estimated cost of $2,400,000. Although this port is the greatest in America, its marine hospital was a hundred years old and so small that some of the patients had to be cared for in an old warehouse. The new building will provide 700 beds. Concurrently, work is being done on seventeen other projects connected with marine hospitals.

Late in 1933 the Public Health Service, along with other Federal agencies, was asked to suggest projects which would provide immediate employment. Four major health undertakings were recommended: (1) an intensive malarial control drainage program in the fourteen States where that malady has been most prevalent; (2) the construction of sanitary privies in small towns and villages and in the unsewered outskirts of larger cities; (3) surveys to determine the extent of typhus fever in rodents, and, (4) the sealing of abandoned coal mines to reduce the acid wastes being discharged into streams.

The vital need for malaria control in many of the southern States was recognized by the Special Board of Public Works, and money for the supervision of the drainage projects was allotted to the Public Health Service. At the same time CWA allocated about 14 mil-

THE STORY OF PWA

lion dollars for the wages of the men who were to dig the ditches. The problem was to strike at the proper places, and these data were supplied by the local health authorities. In many places the Federal work was supplemented by local aid. Ultimately about 10,000 miles of ditches were dug and swamps affecting 12 million persons were drained.

It is too early to speak with any finality on the results of the work, but, in view of our knowledge of the areas covered by the drainage system, it can be conservatively estimated that a saving in health amounting to 100 million dollars a year will be accomplished as long as the ditches are kept clear. It has been calculated that the economic benefit to be derived from the eradication of all malaria will represent a saving to the country of not less than 500 million dollars a year.

It would be difficult to overestimate the importance and value of this drainage work. Malarial infection is responsible for backwardness in school children who, because of the disease, cannot put forth the effort normally expected of them. The loss of energy among adults suffering from malaria is also reflected on the farms and in the industries of the South. The beneficial results of malarial swamp drainage are set forth in a letter received by the Mississippi State Board of Health from one of the plantation owners in the delta. She says:

It occurs to me that you might be interested from a health standpoint in the results of the drainage projects laid out last year on my plantation by Mr. Nelson H. Rector.

In the summer of 1933 I suffered so many losses in manpower and money from long and severe cases of malaria that I wrote Mr. Rector and asked if he would come over and run levels so that I could drain the sloughs and lowlands. Mr. Rector promptly responded, and the levels were run on part of the place. He found that much of our drainage was ineffective and made changes accordingly.

We followed Mr. Rector's program as far as our finances would permit, expecting to complete it gradually. While we were working, the CWA, fortunately for us, came in and dug two of the major ditches included in the program.

As what I consider a direct result of this drainage, we have not had a single case of malaria on that portion of the plantation during the year 1934. My books bear me out in this statement. They do not show one doctor's bill for malaria nor one grain of quinine. Heretofore on this part of the place there has been a constant expense for malaria and resultant maladies.

My books show that tenants on other parts of the place have had usual medical care and quinine for malaria.

We have been fortunate enough to get Mr. Rector to run levels on another portion of the plantation this fall, and Mr. Ogden and I hope to be able to continue the work.

I am writing this letter to you in appreciation of the work you and Mr. Rector have done for me, and I hope that others will avail themselves of the opportunity of this splendid service.

With kindest personal regards, I beg to remain

Cordially yours,

FLORENCE SILLERS OGDEN.

For the second proposal on its list of desirable projects —the construction of sanitary privies—the Public Health Service was allotted $650,000 for supervisory work. The actual construction was done by CWA and FERA workers at a wage cost of 15 million dollars. So far nearly a million sanitary privies have been built in thirty States.

The program was worked out in coöperation with the State health departments and the result, as in the case of malarial swamp drainage, has been to encourage the development of State and local facilities for continuing this work. In many a small town, where it was impractical to extend the sewer system, the local authorities purchased the material and had privies constructed for the homes not serviced by sewers, the cost being liquidated by a service charge. In other places the privies were regarded as a public utility of the city or town.

It is difficult to gauge the benefits to a community from this program in general health and the prevention of disease, but some idea may be gained from the realization that every insanitary privy is both a nuisance and a menace to the homes in its vicinity. The Public Health Service already has been able to calculate some of the good effects from the results in West Virginia. There the State Department of Health began its first concerted effort to control excreta-borne diseases in 1933. Although the program was very limited, deaths from these diseases dropped to the lowest rates in the history of the State. With the inauguration of the CWA program in late 1933, a State-wide campaign got under way. All material was furnished by the owners of the properties on which sanitary improvements were made and all labor was furnished from the relief rolls. From January 1, 1934, to January 31, 1935, 53,000 sanitary privies were constructed in the thickly settled rural areas, including coal-mining villages in which sewage systems were not available.

The popularity of the program is evidenced by the fact that more than thirty-five thousand property owners in the State have recently petitioned the legislature to enact public health laws which will require a sanitary method of excreta disposal at every home in West Virginia, the work to be done at the expense of the property owners when relief labor is no longer available.

The two other points in the program—a study of typhus-carrying rats and the sealing of abandoned coal mines—were also given financial help. Rodent ecto-parasite surveys were made in thirty seaports, and control work was carried on in three southern States. Another group of workers closed the openings of nearly 7,000 mines which were endangering streams with acid discharges.

Even more complicated problems were encountered in the large urban areas. Whenever man has left the comparatively isolated way of living common to hunters and early agriculturists and has begun to build towns and cities, the need for public health measures has appeared. The rough and ready sanitary measures of the lone country dweller would spell destruction in the city. Nor is health the only issue involved. It is certain that life in the United States would not be on so high a level if it were not for the sanitary safeguards we enjoy. Conditions among backward peoples show that ignorance of health matters is accompanied by a lack of cultural progress.

Then there is the economic phase of the city health problem. Leaders in civic affairs and industrialists have learned during the past thirty years that a healthy community is more likely to be a prosperous one. The work of Gorgas and Carter and their associates in cleaning up the Isthmus of Panama did much to bring home to us the monetary value of sanitation and disease control. The measures taken by the Public Health Service in stamping out the rat in San Francisco and New Orleans, thereby preventing a possible epidemic of bubonic plague, saved this country millions of dollars. During the World War the government stressed the necessity for national health, because good health meant efficient fighting men and workers back of the line. The same necessity for good health exists no less in time of peace.

The problem of sewage, crucial as it is in the country and the small town, is magnified many times in the city. In many parts of the country, the cities draw their water supply from nearby rivers which, in times of extreme drought, become low and sluggish. During these periods the sewage discharged into the streams is not carried off promptly and the natural purifying process characteristic of water in normal flow is incomplete. Often cities obtain water from streams utilized by industrial plants to carry off deleterious waste material. There always has been a conflict between the necessity for the disposal of sewage and industrial waste and that of maintaining a stream in as pure a condition as possible for a domestic water supply.

In many localities, a typical river basin suffers pollution from many sources. Usually above the city there is a deforested area on either bank, the timber having been sacrificed for lumber, with the result that soil erosion fills the river with mud. Then may come an abandoned mine, from which seep sulphur and acid waste. Next there are factories and a factory town, adding their pollution to the already impure water, and, finally, there is the local metropolis emptying huge sewer mains into the current.

Even though the filtration plants may overcome most

of the danger connected with the use of such water for drinking purposes, it is wasteful and unpleasant to permit such a river condition to exist. What might be an asset of great natural beauty and of real usefulness becomes nothing more or less than an open sewer; neighboring communities which depend upon wells for their water are actually endangered and the expense of purification by the cities and towns is burdensome.

Intending, so far as possible, to help bring about water purification both through sewage projects and filtration systems, PWA had allocated, by January 1, 1935, about 241 million dollars for this purpose. Nearly 149 millions were assigned to sewage projects; about five millions to combination sewer and water system projects; approximately 82 millions to water systems, and slightly more than 5 millions for garbage and rubbish disposal plants. By April 1, 1935, close to 29 million man-hours of work had been provided at the sites of these projects, while probably as many more had been created through the fabrication and transportation of the materials used.

The most interesting of the projects of this type is that of the Sanitary District of Chicago, which would not have been possible except for the intelligent coöperation of Ross A. Woodhull, then one of the trustees of the district and now its president. For many years the metropolitan district of Chicago had been emptying raw sewage into the Chicago River whence it flowed through a drainage canal into the Illinois and then into the Mississippi River. So as to insure a water flow adequate to purify partially the sewage and carry it away, large quantities of water were being let into the Chicago River out of Lake Michi-

gan. Other Great Lakes States objected that such a use of
the water was lowering the level of the lakes and thus
infringing upon their rights. After protracted litigation,
the Supreme Court of the United States determined that
the diversion of water from Lake Michigan by the district
should be reduced to a maximum of 1,500 cubic feet per
second by December 31, 1938.

This allowance, it was quickly determined by sanitary
engineers, would be insufficient to carry away the raw
sewage collected in the drainage canal. They recommended that disposal plants be built to avert the disease
and annoyance that were inevitable as soon as the water
diversion was curtailed. Work on these plants was started,
but the depression and the so-called tax strike in Chicago
forced a halt when the enterprise was only half completed. To add to its difficulties, about this time the
district was compelled to default on its bonds. Such was
the position of the Sanitary District when it applied for
a PWA loan and grant late in 1933.

Soon after the request was received, we were flooded
with protesting letters from Chicago citizens who maintained that it would be folly to entrust the sanitary officials with such a large sum of money as they were asking
for. The writers pointed out that the record of this particular body had been worse than dubious in the past, a
circumstance that was already within the personal knowledge of the Administrator of PWA. These warnings, the
fact that I come from the village of Winnetka which is in
the Sanitary District, and the undoubtedly tangled financial affairs of the District, caused us to exercise unusual
care in considering this loan.

We said that we would advance approximately 42 million dollars in the form of a loan, but that because of the tangled financial affairs of the District and the protests based on its past performance, we would withhold the usual grant covering 30 per cent of the cost of labor and material until the job was completed to the satisfaction of PWA. Satisfactory completion of the work would cause us to make the grant, about 14 million dollars in this case, and would thus reduce the District's debt to PWA to 28 million dollars. This unusual contract later proved to be a very useful club when it was necessary to bring pressure against the Sanitary District.

We also made a careful study of the District's engineering plans. A commission, consisting of Joshua D'Esposito, Chicago engineer, General Charles W. Kutz, Professor Daniel W. Mead of the University of Wisconsin, and William K. Storey, former president and chief engineer of the Santa Fé Railroad, was appointed to make sure that the project was set up as economically as possible. Exhaustive hearings on the plans were held and the commission finally proposed changes and modifications which would make it possible to accomplish almost twice as much work with the same amount of money.

At the same time PWA's legal department discovered a gross inequality between the taxes paid by the packing industry to the District, and that industry's use of the District's sewage facilities. One of the principal reasons why it was necessary to construct such an expensive treatment plant as was proposed was the extremely heavy use of the sewers by the packers—a use equivalent to that of a domestic population of two million persons. Yet the packers' taxes were relatively small and had been for many years.

There is no sewer rental system in Chicago, but the Illinois statutes permit the Sanitary District to enter into contracts with extraordinary users, charging them rates proportionate to the quantity of their trade waste. A number of years ago when plans for the new sewage plants were conceived, the District attempted to send inspectors into the packing plants to study their wastes and the cost of treatment, but an injunction was sought to bar the way. The District supinely allowed the court hearing on the issues to be postponed indefinitely. The politicians preferred to let the people as a whole pay for the sewage services rendered to the great packing industry rather than to press a just suit against selfish but powerful interests. So before we allocated the money asked for, we insisted that the District do two things:

1. Appoint special counsel, to be approved by the Administrator, to prosecute vigorously its action against the packers to permit inspection of the plants.

2. Procure additional legislation which would permit the levying of sewage treatment taxes upon all extraordinary users of the system, if existing legislation should prove not to be sufficient.

The packers saw that we meant business and graciously entered into an arrangement which permitted representatives of the District, under PWA supervision, to study their trade wastes. It was understood that the packers would decide later either to use the District's facilities by payment of a service charge, or build their own disposal plants.

Still another flaw in the past record of the District was

found by PWA and a change in methods demanded. The District owned locks on the drainage canal, and considerable electric power was being generated at those locks. Most of the time, except in periods of excessive rainfall when an especially large quantity of power is needed by the District to pump water, there was a surplus of electricity. A part of this the District had been "selling" to the city of Chicago. I use this word to describe this transaction, but perhaps I should rather use "billing" because the city, although it always scrupulously paid bills rendered by privately owned utilities, did not trouble itself to pay the District a cent on a debt which, when the application for the loan was made, had reached the astounding sum of 7 million dollars.

About half of this sum was represented by a judgment that had been obtained several years earlier by the Sanitary District against the city. Soon after this judgment was secured the legislature provided for the levying by the city of a special tax to pay off outstanding judgments. The money collected was used to meet the more recent but apparently the far more important and valid judgments of private interests for which the city government had a greater regard than it had for the taxpayers of the Sanitary District.

We insisted that legislation be secured to provide for the payment by the city of judgments in the order of their rendition, and now funds are being collected by Chicago out of this special tax to pay what it owes the Sanitary District. At the same time, in order to make the city realize that it must meet current bills from the District, I was forced to warn both Chicago and the District that the allocation would be rescinded if power bills were again allowed to pile up. The result was that last year, with the coöperation of Mayor Edward J. Kelly, the city paid to the District in cash and tax warrants all of its current power bill amounting to some $700,000.

Even after these and other matters had been straightened out, we never relaxed our vigilance. During all of the construction on this project, PWA inspectors have been on the job, and their careful supervision has saved the taxpapers many thousands of dollars. One example, relating to the faulty construction of a section of a sewer, three-fifths of a mile in length, has already been cited.

In Chicago, except in the jaundiced opinion of certain snarling opponents of all that the New Deal stands for, there is little doubt that PWA has been of great benefit to the people. The use of Federal funds has made possible the construction of this and other works necessary to ensure the health and well-being of the citizens and at the same time employment has been provided at one of the great centers of unemployment. The Sanitary District, under the capable management of President Woodhull, is now conducting its affairs in a businesslike manner and on a cash basis. With our aid and advice, its plans have been changed so as to save many millions of dollars to the sorely beset taxpayers.

The following letter is yet another testimonial of the appreciation that has come from all directions of the intangible benefits which have accompanied the very material improvements resulting from the expenditure of PWA funds:

CITY OF SAUK CENTRE

Minnesota

Office of L. L. Kells, City Attorney

February 15, 1935.

Fred Schilplin,

St. Cloud, Minnesota.

My dear Fred:

The final payment of Federal Grant has been delivered to Sauk Centre in connection with our PWA Sewage Treatment plant.

You will recall that I was somewhat skeptical as to the benefits of PWA and felt that the technicalities involved made a grant hardly worthwhile.

I still feel that Sauk Centre was required to furnish much technical information which served no good purpose; however, it may be that under some circumstances it would be beneficial and necessary.

On the whole I feel that PWA required much better performance on the part of the contractor than we would have been able to do unassisted; that PWA, having no local connections, was able to lay down requirements which we could not have done, and that the contractor complied with such requirements much more readily than he would have done had the enforcement been attempted by the city or its engineers.

I have sent our thanks to Mr. Carey for the way in which he has handled the matter. He has been consistently courteous and helpful and has been patient in hearing and explaining all of our questions and demands. I feel that he has carried out his duties on the high plane on which we fondly expect government officials to perform, but in which expectation we are so often disappointed.

State Board of Health engineers tell me that we have a very well constructed and efficient plant. Engineers for the State Board of Control have also inspected the plant in connection with an appropriation to cover treatment of sewage from the Minnesota Home School for Girls and they likewise approve of both the plan and the construction, so I feel that we have a very good job.

Thank you for the courtesies and consideration which you extended to us in connection with this matter.

Yours very truly,

(signed) L. L. KELLS,

City Attorney.

In order to determine whether or not these types of projects were furthering the main objective of PWA—putting men to work—the Department of Labor conducted an inquiry into the economic results of expenditures on water and sewage projects. It reports that an analysis of sixteen completed water and sewage projects financed by Public Works Administration loans and grants reveals that 26.3 per cent of the contract price was paid to labor on the job; that manufacturers of materials received orders to account for 50.4 per cent; and that 23.3 per cent went for profit and overhead. This overhead includes such items as salaries of office workers, rent, insurance, workmen's compensation, depreciation of equipment, etc., and profit.

Chapter IX

SLUMS TO DECENT HOMES

Twice a week, on Mondays and Thursdays, around a table in the Interior Building, a group of men discuss one of the most significant phases of PWA's program. These men are serious; they waste no time in getting down to business; they speak briefly and to the point. They are the efficient administrative officers of a great enterprise who are making use of the effective weapon of technical co-ordination in the fight the government has undertaken to replace noisome slums with low-rent housing.

Seated in the room are the branch chiefs of the Housing Division of PWA. Rubbing shoulders are architects, demolition experts, real-estate authorities, building contractors, apartment managers and lawyers, all working harmoniously on the really intricate problem of low-cost housing. The uncommonness of the group becomes apparent when it is realized that never before has housing been considered as one complete process from land acquisition to apartment management.

To understand why the group around the table has attacked the housing problem in this new way; to appreciate why it is working so hard and seriously, it is necessary to consider the problem of slums and low-cost housing in the United States to-day.

178

We have long been in agreement that slums are a disgrace to our country. We are familiar with the long list of their disabilities—impure and insufficient water supply; insanitary toilets, if any; lack of sewer connections; overcrowding; want of light; inadequate heat and ventilation; excessive dampness and absence of screening against flies and mosquitoes; an environment of vice and crime. Such areas are a heavy liability against the whole community. They pile up extra costs on account of the extra policing they require, the added fire protection and health service they need, and the additional expense to which they put us for courts and penal institutions. Slums breed disease and harbor epidemics; they spawn crime and nurture gangsters.

We have learned much about the slums in many cities since our housing division set out upon its Augean task. Most of us had heard about New York's "Hell's Kitchen," but our investigators and specialists have become intimately acquainted with the "Arks" of Memphis and New Orleans—jumbled two-story structures with sixteen or more Negro families on each floor, drawing water from a spigot in the same muddy yard where the common privy is found. From there it is only a short journey to the "Corrals" of San Antonio, where as many as eight or ten persons live in one room. Other dreadful rookeries are the "Monkey's Nest" of Youngstown and the "Bandbox" houses of Philadelphia, not to overlook those local areas which any of us could cite from his own city wherever it may be. Nor does one have to go to a city to find slums. In all parts of the Nation, our countrysides are dotted with them.

Another aspect of this question is that the slum dweller pays more proportionately for what he gets than the man who lives in a more desirable dwelling. While his rent may seem low in actual dollars and cents, it is high when one considers what that rent pays for—insanitary, often sunless and airless, quarters in a dilapidated old building which may be yielding its owner all of twenty or twenty-five per cent upon its actual value.

And if the slum dweller pays more than he should for rent, he also pays extra for everything he buys. The grocer and butcher who serve slum neighborhoods, like their customers, are paying exorbitant rents on the basis of the value of the premises occupied by them. These rents have to be figured, and legitimately so, as part of the cost of the goods they sell over their counters. So will it be seen that the cost of the slums is high from every point of view—economic as well as social and moral.

They are so costly, when you come to think of it, that it is a matter of surprise that a supposedly prudent and businesslike people should so long have endured these unsightly and objectionable warrens in which we have forced men and women to make their homes. On a dollar and cents basis alone, there is nothing we could do that would be so worth while as the complete eradication of slums everywhere in the land.

We call it a subsidy for the government to invest some of its money in this worthiest of social enterprises, but in fact it is no subsidy at all. Clean out the slums and we would have to pay less for police and fire protection. There would be a diminution of vice and crime. Tuberculosis and other preventable and communicable diseases

America's first low-rent housing program was launched under PWA—one of the projects.

that levy such a heavy toll upon the health and lives of people living together under crowded and insanitary conditions would be reduced to a minimum. Instead of turning out semi-invalids, youths broken down by disease or vice before they reach their maturity, we would develop normal, healthy men and women who, so far from being a burden upon the State, would be both able and willing to pull their own weight in the boat. Money spent to eradicate slums is a sound and safe investment in citizenship, in character, in health; an investment that for all time to come will pay rich dividends in the form of happier and more worth-while lives.

Some people, in speaking of the government's interest in low-rent housing, seem to have confused PWA's program with that of the Federal Housing Administration. Actually there is no basis for confusion between the two. The Federal Housing Administration contemplates renovating, repairing and adding to existing homes. It has been difficult, ever since the 1929 crash, for the home owner to borrow money on a mortgage. A man may be able to support his family and pay his taxes and insurance, but still lack the capital necessary to put on a new roof, build a bathroom, or add an extra wing to his home. He can make payments at a reasonable rate of interest over a period of years, but he is unable to make a present investment. So the Federal Government steps in through the Federal Housing Administration and guarantees the loan.

Likewise, there are those who have the desire to build new homes of their own. In existing circumstances, banks or lending institutions may hesitate to accept a mortgage on the undertaking. Here, too, the Federal Housing Administration is able to aid by insuring the mortgage.

This is a fine and worth-while undertaking, but it is distinct and apart from the problem of cleaning out the slums and building low-rental homes for those in the lowest income classes who never have had any credit at the bank and who, if they had to provide an equity even in prosperous times as an inducement to a bank to lend money, would never be able to own their own homes. Such countries as Great Britain, Austria, Germany and Italy, which, in the matter of housing, are far ahead of the richest and most enterprising country in the world, have discovered and frankly admit that slums cannot be eradicated except on the basis of a government subsidy. We in this country must be realists on this subject. I believe that every American family is entitled to decent living conditions—to light, to air, to sunshine, to clean streets, to healthful surroundings, to an absence of preventable fire hazards, to parks and playgrounds in order to give the children now playing among noxious garbage cans in filthy alleys a chance to grow into normal and healthful American citizens.

If such a home cannot be provided without a subsidy from the government, then I, for one, am for a subsidy.

We have encountered grave difficulties in getting our slum-clearance program under way. It was natural, but unfortunate, that in staffing our housing division we turned in the first instance to those who were considered experts because they were eloquent in explaining the theory of low-rent housing. We discovered, to our cost, after an irreparable loss of precious time, that too often they had no practical experience at all. As soon as this fact became clear, a reorganization was promptly effected. I sought out in Chicago a man experienced in building, who was known to me to possess drive and energy and force of character. Colonel Horatio B. Hackett was persuaded to come to Washington and accept the responsible post of director of the housing division.

Under the first director of housing, it was thought that the low-rent problem could be solved by private initiative, that limited dividend groups, borrowing 85 per cent of their capital from PWA, could build and operate their own projects. Private interests were invited to undertake the construction of low-cost homes. More than 500 applications were received, but only a few merited serious attention. Many were frank attempts to sell the government vacant land in high tax areas, while others were of a purely speculative nature. It quickly became obvious that our much vaunted private initiative, as so often happens when the goal is a social good instead of a private profit, was unable or unwilling to undertake the job.

After considerable fussing with limited-dividend projects, a few of which were approved at the instance of various groups of private citizens, it was decided that the housing division would do its own constructing and operating. After Colonel Hackett was placed in charge, the division proceeded to execute a right wheel, almost a right-about face, and moved forward with its Federal program.

The working out of the necessary new technique was slow. We had to learn by experimentation the most effective methods of assembling land. We were not satisfied to take the first that was offered at the price asked; the cost of land is too vital a factor in the rent to be charged to permit such reckless business methods. We were called upon to determine the most economical methods of construction, the best materials for our purposes. We had to dicker with city councils, with social agencies, with racial groups. We were determined to keep our feet on the ground, to build soundly rather than hastily, to the end that what we produced would be true low-rental housing. To produce well-wrought housing would be to lay the foundations for a really comprehensive housing program for this Nation; to act precipitately and ill-advisedly would be to create a faulty, expensive product which by its inevitable failure would weigh down low-cost housing in the United States for many years.

There are some who apparently would have us produce housing, hasty-pudding fashion, over night. Some enthusiasts impatiently refuse to admit the variety and the magnitude of the problems confronting the government in its endeavors to institute low-rent housing in our cities. Others, seeing in the housing movement merely an opportunity for profit for themselves, are as impatient as the theorists at even reasonable delays. They want their profits and they want them quickly—that is the extent of their interest. Still another group has only the vaguest possible impression of what it wants or how to go about getting it. But it, too, wants the Federal Government to do something about something and do it quickly.

But we are more interested in results than in theories. We recognize our responsibility to complete the task at hand as rapidly, but also in as workmanlike a manner, as possible. But we have an even greater responsibility to the ideal of slum clearance itself. We want what we do to be so creditably done that no one in the United States can doubt that it is not only possible but desirable to clean out our reeking slums. We would be doing a disservice to the principle of slum clearance if, yielding to the uninformed criticism of feet-on-desk critics, we should permit ourselves to produce results so badly conceived, so wretchedly planned and so flimsily built that the effect would be to discredit for a generation to come what seems to me to be the most desirable social objective toward which the government is moving at this time.

To make our projects self-liquidating and at the same time keep rentals low, calls for great ingenuity on the part of our architects, builders and managers. It also requires minimum costs for land. I have no apologies to make for keeping such costs down. It is apparent to all but the wilfully blind that prudence must be exercised in obtaining property. Careful work on the part of our land-accumulation branch and our inspection division has made possible in many instances the acquisition of sites by friendly negotiations at prices which will permit low-cost results. Condemnation proceedings have had to be resorted to principally as a method of clearing title.

Our care in keeping down our land costs has called for more sneers from those who clear slums between courses at conference luncheons than any other part of our program. Those who cavil are above such vulgar practices as bargaining for land until the lowest possible price can be obtained. They are especially indignant that careful appraisements should be made by experts and that investigators should be sent out to check on figures that seem too high. They refer to this operation as "falling over Mr. Glavis' investigators." Some of these critics for so many years have impressed themselves and their friends with their profound and exclusive knowledge on the subject of housing that they seem to fear that they will lose their vogue if slum clearance in this country is actually brought down out of the clouds and placed firmly on terra firma, where it belongs. It all goes to prove the danger of toying too long with a naked idea. The man who makes this mistake is likely, too late, to discover that he has merely become futile.

Once it had rolled up its sleeves and descended from the ivory tower of meditation and theory to the reality of the architect's workroom, the housing division began to make remarkable progress. By January 1, 1935, low-rent housing projects were going ahead vigorously in many cities.

When we really got to work on the problem we found that the architect for each project was spending most of his time in an attempt to work out efficient interlocking apartment units. One architect reported that more than three-fifths of his time had been devoted to this phase of the work whereas it should have been spent on simplifying these units into a workable site plan.

The housing division took the position that the interlocking units would be much the same for each project as they would of necessity be governed by certain factors. It thereupon set out to determine of what the most efficient units should consist.

Starting with the fundamental requirements of safety, health and comfort, research was carried on so as to arrive at what seemed to be the best solution within given price limits. The study of existing conditions proved that fire-proof construction, particularly in buildings over two stories in height, was most useful. In fact, the present procedure is to have practically all one- and two-story buildings fireproof, not only for reasons of ready evacuation in the event of fire, but also to increase the normal expectancy of life of the building. It is known that fire-proof materials have far longer lasting qualities than non-fireproof. Safety therefore was approached principally through the transition of construction from non-fireproof to fireproof.

In the slum dwellings studied, it was found that health was left to take care of itself so far as any improvements were concerned. In the typical "railroad flat," which is the name given to the dwellings in which the rooms are strung in a line from the front of the building to the rear, the only two rooms receiving direct light are those at the extreme front and the extreme rear; the other four or five rooms in between either receive no light at all or, at best, an inadequate amount from a four-foot light court. It was discovered that the kitchen sink acted as the one convenience in the entire unit as a source of water supply, and included among its many functions dish-washing, bathing and laundry. In most cases there was found to be a single water-closet in a windowless chamber in the center of the building, which served all apartments on that floor.

For the housing division projects, a brand-new scheme has been adopted, aiming for health without extra costs or waste of space. It was decided to utilize for building purposes not more than 30 per cent of the total land area of any one project, leaving 70 per cent for such developments as parks, lawns, walks, drives and playgrounds. With these objects in mind it was determined that typical solutions would have to be arrived at that would cover not only site plans but individual plan units as well. It was with this idea in mind that the typical plan units as later developed by the housing division were originally created.

The rooms heretofore built in tenement houses and flat-house units were mere cubicles. They bear no evidence of any consideration for the placing of furniture or for the inter-relationship of rooms with respect to privacy or use, such as the relationship of the dining room to the kitchen. Exposures were completely ignored and the room facing the street, which was, of course, the noisest one, was considered to be the choice location. These defects have been remedied in making up our unit plans; and the comfort and well-being of the tenant is our prime consideration.

The creation of these typical or sample unit plans was a big forward step in the movement for better housing in this country. They provide a basis for all future work. It must be remembered that low-rent housing is a brand-new subject in the architect's curriculum. There are no precedents to guide him except the attempts made in recent years in Europe and these are of slight value for our purposes because of our different conditions.

The unit plan may be defined as a dwelling unit or group of dwelling units combined into a compact mass by means of carefully adjusted interlocking spaces. It avoids unnecessary waste, meanwhile availing itself of every sound fundamental of proper planning. As a starting point, the minimum size of rooms was determined both as to area as well as to dimensions. Equipment was also pre-determined. For example, incinerators were adopted for use in all apartment-house units rather than dumbwaiters. The unit plan as worked out covers only one floor but the units may be stacked one directly upon the other, thereby creating an apartment house of the desired number of stories in height.

There is little danger of over-standardization because of these unit plans. Already over forty-five have been completed, covering almost every conceivable type of better-housing project. At the same time, no architect is forced to use our plans if he can submit something that achieves the same result as well or better. We merely offer ours as a starting point in the hope that they can be improved upon. If the architect is satisfied with these units, however, he is free to spend more time developing a proper site plan.

We have not limited our planning to the apartment units, but have extended it to provide for the recreation and community life of the tenants. In coöperation with duly constituted local governmental units and authorized agencies, a study will be made in each community to determine the extent of existing facilities and the possibilities of their improvement and utilization.

Based upon this investigation a program will be developed to make available to our tenants the best recreational facilities and community leadership obtainable. In the development of this plan, provision will be made for the many different types of facilities which may be needed, such as schools, parks, playgrounds, swimming pools and community buildings, the latter of which may include auditoriums, gymnasiums and club rooms. Those facilities for leisure time activities which normally center in the community should be provided and operated by local agencies at no cost to the housing project. Leisure time activities which normally center in the home will be provided by us and must be carried by the rents. Wherever the housing division builds, it keeps in mind these social factors, as well as the more strictly architectural ones.

Of the seven limited-dividend projects of the program, most of which were started before the "about-face," of the division, three were occupied, three were actually being built and one was preparing to go into construction on April 1, 1935. The allotments for these projects which will provide 3,401 living units totaled $10,971,600.

On April 1, 1935, thirteen Federal projects were in various stages of actual progress in New York, Chicago, Atlanta, Cleveland, Indianapolis, Cincinnati, Detroit, Montgomery and Louisville. For these projects, condemnation of land had been started or sites were in course of acquisition except in Louisville, where a Federal District Court had enjoined further purchases. This suit is now pending on appeal in the United States Circuit Court of Appeals. Slums had actually been torn down in Atlanta, Cleveland, Indianapolis and Montgomery. These thirteen projects, together with the balance available for New York City, involve a total expenditure of more than 80 million dollars and will supply nearly 20,000 living units.

By the same date we had authorized sixteen additional projects at a cost of $30,821,000. The locations of these have not been announced, but surveys have been completed and options are now being taken. These will provide 8,240 more living units.

Preliminary work has been completed on twenty other projects, which can be put through promptly when funds are available. These will cost $39,128,000 and supply approximately 11,000 additional living units. All of the 150 million dollar fund allocated to date for housing has been obligated, and the projects actually under way, in addition to those approved and ready for approval, will provide more than 42,000 individual dwellings.

Housing under the Administration's program is intended to be self-liquidating. With the exception of the 30 per cent grant, authorized by Congress for certain PWA projects, the money used in financing this low-cost housing will be returned to the Treasury through the collection of rents.

Another housing activity, made possible by PWA funds, is that of the division of subsistence homesteads, under the Department of the Interior. Comprising more than a simple provision for dwellings, this program has a threefold object: the decentralization of industry; the opening up of congested factory areas, and a demonstration of the social benefits of a sound community life based on a combination of part-time industrial employment and small-scale farming. As its name implies, the subsistence homesteads program contemplates the establishment of homes upon plots of land sufficiently large to grow a major portion of the food required by the homestead family.

Through the division of subsistence homesteads, the

government buys the land, constructs modern houses and
necessary outbuildings, purchases live stock and agricultural machinery, provides roads and water and other
utilities and then sells the individual homesteads, properly
equipped, upon a thirty-year payment plan with interest
at three per cent. The selection of homesteaders is intended to be limited to families with annual incomes of
less than $1,200, who come from crowded industrial
areas, or who have been driven from such areas by the
depression.

In size, individual homesteads vary from the acre or
two of the worker's garden type to from twenty to thirty
acres in more rural projects. Houses range from three to
six rooms in size and cost from $1,500 to $3,000. The
purchase price includes in most cases essential farming
and gardening equipment, seeds and fertilizer, a small
flock of chickens, a pig or two, and possibly a cow, a
horse or a mule.

From its inception, the subsistence homesteading program has been experimental. The 25 million dollars
designated by Congress to undertake the work, while it is
impressive, is little more than a limited research fund
when it is compared with the magnitude of the field for
this new enterprise. Even before the depression large
numbers of workers were employed on a part-time basis.
Technological advances presage more part-time employment as well as unemployment, yet thousands of persons
on farms are constantly moving into urban areas in the
futile hope of securing jobs. Or were, before 1929.
Subsistence homesteading promises a way to check this
movement by demonstrating the economic and social

value of a way of life in which a limited earned cash income may be supplemented by produce from the land for household use.

Frankly experimental, as I have said, as a new venture in the field of social endeavor, the program has experienced the vicissitudes common to the laboratory and the testing ground. Experiments have been undertaken with portable houses and health insurance, with homesteaders' coöperatives and community education. Some of the undertakings have not worked out; others have been successful; but all have been valuable in determining policies which will provide a sound basis for the future development of the program, and for the undertaking of similar experiments by States, municipalities and private interests that will be inspired, it is hoped, to follow the government's example.

An optimism that grew out of an undervaluation of the manifold problems involved has been succeeded by a realistic understanding of the many intriguing difficulties that lie in the way. Critics have been scornful because happy homesteaders did not, like Cadmus' soldiers, spring out of the ground over night.

The establishment of a subsistence homestead is not simply a matter of building a cheap home in the country. To study a proposed project site; to draw up sound plans and outline a budget which will come within the financial ability of the homesteader to make repayment; to determine the fertility of the proposed land and the sufficiency of the title to it; to provide roads, water, electricity, and sewage disposal; to select homesteaders who need help, and who will make the most of the help given them; to build houses that will outlast the thirty-year amortization period—these steps require time and preparation.

The division, on April 1, 1935, had on its list some sixty-four approved projects, of which forty-five had been announced publicly. Of these forty-five, house construction is in progress on a score of projects and land improvement work is under way on practically all of the remainder. When completed, the projects already approved will accommodate approximately 6,500 homesteaders, and the total cost will be close to 19 million dollars. Some 1,200 houses are under construction and about the same number of homestead families have been selected.

The Public Works Administration will continue its program for better homes in city and country so long as it has the necessary funds. The vaunted standard of living of the American people requires that we substitute decent housing for filthy slums wherever they may be found. Such a program will accomplish a great social good as well as stimulate the whole construction industry and provide work for great numbers of people.

Chapter X

MEN AT WORK

I F Thomas Jefferson were alive to-day, he might want to rewrite for a second time the famous English declaration of man's right to enjoy "life, liberty and property." In Philadelphia, during that unbearably hot summer when the founding fathers were drafting the Declaration of Independence, Jefferson amplified the word "property" into "the pursuit of happiness." It is quite conceivable that now he would want to modernize his language and cause the Declaration to affirm the right of every man to life, liberty and the pursuit of a gainful occupation.

Only during the past few years have we seen how closely bound together are happiness and work. At the present time lack of work, resulting in widespread unemployment, is a national problem. We see on every side the physical and mental havoc wrought by joblessness upon every class of men and their families. We see the results of crippling malnutrition and spiritual disintegration; we see the subtle moral enervation caused by doles.

The pursuit of happiness meant to Jefferson, among other things, the right of a man to work in his own interest at a job within his capacity and to his liking. There were jobs for all then; plenty of them. That there should be such a problem as unemployment was inconceivable.

195

Accordingly, with the colonies gasping for man power, it never occurred to the framers of the Constitution to go a step further and assert man's right to have an opportunity to work. A picture of a nation with one-fifth of its male population unable to find work would have been considered, in those days of underproduction, as preposterous as a description of a thirty-five-passenger airplane.

Yet, although the thought has not been expressly stated either in the Declaration of Independence or the Constitution, there has been a long-standing American tradition that work at a living wage should be available to every individual who wants to work. I am old-fashioned enough to wish to preserve this tradition, and I am modern enough to be willing to use the power of government, if necessary, to ensure that such a fine ideal shall not pass from our national life.

The efforts of the Public Works Administration have been directed toward the preservation of this tradition by the use of governmental power. The true test of the success of these efforts depends, I am sure, not only upon the beauty or usefulness of the projects undertaken but also upon the amount of work provided by them. The figures which follow will show, I confidently believe, that PWA has been a success, up to the limits of its capacity, in accomplishing what it was designed to accomplish.

To explain adequately the effect our program has had upon the national economic life, it is necessary to recall the important position held by the construction industry before 1930. Building was being done in every section of the country and the resulting demand for materials supplied work for many other industries. In the good years

"Off Relief Rolls—on to Pay Rolls."

one worker out of every twenty was employed on construction, and for every worker employed directly at the site, at least one other was employed in factory, office, mine or on the railroads.

The depression brought construction to a standstill First to lose their jobs were the construction men, the masons, bricklayers, carpenters, steel workers, electricians, plumbers and decorators. Later, for each man thrown out of work at the site, at least one other lost his job further back along the line.

But this direct and primary indirect unemployment, serious as it was, marked only the beginning of the vicious circle. Within a few months of the time that construction began to slump, there was a decline in secondary indirect employment. The clothing, automotive, radio and other industries, whose existence depends upon the buying power of the mason and the decorator, the mine worker and the factory hand, exhibited symptoms of unhealth. As they reduced production, more men were laid off, new circles were started.

Now let us examine the distribution of work caused by PWA's program. The uninitiated is always surprised to learn that public works, with a few minor exceptions, have been built by private enterprise. Private contractors do the building; private industry receives the orders for machinery, materials and transportation. The great bridges being thrown across San Francisco Bay provide work not alone for private individuals in California; they have caused orders to be placed in steel mills in Colorado and Pennsylvania; they have required lumber from the forests of Oregon and Washington; they have provided thousands of freight loads for the railroads; they have called for cement and stone from many other quarters. Our money has bought employment almost entirely.

There has been some misunderstanding about our expenditures and I should like to emphasize that PWA money has gone for three things: profits, the purchase of land, and employment. Now the profits have been rigorously limited not only by competitive bidding by contractors and material men, but also by our own careful supervision of the projects. From the first it has been our policy that only a very small proportion of any allocation should go for the purchase of property. Some land, of course, is necessary for almost every project but we have kept this expenditure down to a minimum in order that as much as possible might go for labor.

It is a conservative estimate that 70 to 80 per cent of practically every construction project allotment goes for wages. In many cases the proportion is higher. A large part of the confusion on this subject is due to the arbitrary division of labor into direct and indirect classifications. Merely for convenience we have distinguished between direct, or labor on the actual site of the project, and indirect, or "behind the line" labor in the mills, mines, factories and on the railroads, which turn out and transport the material that is used in the actual construction.

Now, who is to say which is the most important—the laborer who pours the cement at the dam, the one who digs the limestone in the quarry, or the one who hauls the finished product? As a matter of fact, they are all of equal importance. In all three cases they are usually workmen who, if it were not for the PWA program, would be unemployed and probably on the relief rolls. They are likewise all, as a rule, employed by private contractors no matter on which part of the work they are engaged. So, obviously, PWA is giving employment all down the line and any distinction between direct and indirect labor is both misleading and unimportant, so far as total employment and general economic benefits are concerned.

Adding together the number of jobs filled through the United States Employment Service, the probable number taken by men supplied through labor unions and men called back to work by the railroad loans, it is believed that somewhere in the neighborhood of 2 million construction site jobs were opened up by the public works program between July 1, 1933, and January 1, 1935.

Some of these jobs were permanent; others lasted but a few days. Many men have had jobs on several projects. In August, 1933, when PWA was just getting under way, 4,699 men were employed; by August of 1934, this number had increased to 602,581. Throughout 1934 an average of 500,000 men was steadily at work at construction sites.

The amount of direct employment has varied considerably according to the type of project. The greatest amount of direct employment was on those types of projects for which the least amount of indirect labor was necessary. For instance, a million dollars spent for roads employed, on the average, 7,922 men for one month on the site, whereas the average employment for a million dollars used for engineering structures, such as bridges and tunnels, was only 3,995 men for one month. Obviously the indirect labor needed for road construction is much less than that required for complicated engineering structures, and probably lower than for any other important type of public works.

If we use the very conservative average figure of three on indirect for everyone on direct employment, the reckoning is that PWA has kept approximately two million persons at normal productive work. When the families of these men are taken into consideration, the figures loom much larger and considerably increase the number of persons saved from relief rolls.

In its construction program PWA has given employment at the site to supervisors, architects, engineers, skilled and unskilled workers. Indirectly it has helped those engaged in (1) the distribution of materials through wholesale and retail agencies; (2) the transportation of materials and supplies; (3) the manufacture of materials; and (4) the extraction of raw materials from mines, quarries and forests. Further it aided in the production of consumer goods which were purchased with the wages distributed in the course of the other processes.

All kinds of labor have benefited from the program, skilled, semi-skilled and unskilled of many and varied trades. During November of 1934, the Bureau of Labor Statistics of the Department of Labor calculated that on non-Federal public works projects, the proportion was 38 per cent unskilled, 18 per cent semi-skilled and 44 per cent skilled. During the same month, the average hourly wages paid to these three classes throughout the country were $1.225 to skilled, 72.2 cents to semi-skilled and 51.5 cents to unskilled.

A suspension tower for the Davenport, Iowa, bridge nears completion. This project is being constructed with a loan and grant allotment of $1,527,400 from the Public Works Administration. It is estimated that it will provide 3,600 man-months of employment.

Workers have been obtained from either the United States Employment Service of the Department of Labor or the local trade union headquarters. In many cases they were employees who were reëngaged by their old employers. Between July, 1933, and December 31, 1934, nearly two and a quarter million applicants for work were certified to construction site jobs by the Employment Service. During the same period, several hundred thousand additional construction site jobs were filled by men hired through local unions.

Most of the men cleared through the Employment Service were unskilled laborers with no union affiliations. On union jobs, the men were obtained by contractors through the recognized local unions, and, on non-union jobs, through the Employment Service.

An example of the importance of public works to a stranded community is that of a small town in Florida. I have a report from a town in that State with a population of about three thousand. "On January 1, 1934," the report reads, "there were in the town approximately six hundred persons on the relief roll. Business in general was stagnant and the merchants and other business men were wondering where the money for the next month's rent, or the next grocery bill was coming from. The people had, to some extent, lost interest and were in somewhat of a 'panicky' frame of mind."

This was the condition until the Public Works Administration made a loan and grant of $1,500,000 for a much-needed bridge. Work was started on the bridge in May of 1934. Four hundred workmen were needed and three hundred and fifty were employed from the town. By

November the weekly payrolls averaged approximately $7,500. Immediately the town assumed a new aspect; business began to flourish again; more people were attracted to the town and the surrounding region took on an air of prosperity. The relief rolls were reduced from six hundred to one hundred persons, none of whom was qualified to work. "In other words," the report goes on to say, "this number is about the normal load of relief cases for a community of this size."

The lifting of this sick community back to a healthy and vigorous life illustrates clearly the benefits of public works throughout the country. In the larger cities where complex influences are at work the rôle played by any one agency in the recovery program is hard to follow. But it may safely be said that the story of the small Florida town has been repeated in thousands of other American communities in varying degrees.

Nor has the effect of PWA been felt only where projects were actually under way. Hundreds of towns and thousands of factories were benefited, perhaps without realizing that PWA was the cause. As orders for material came in, new help was needed and sometimes new machinery, which in turn caused other employment in some other factory. All of the men and women recalled to work in these establishments were once more able to buy clothes and food for their families. The factories and farmers producing these articles took on new life and needed more help. Accordingly unemployment was again reduced and more people thus enabled to resume their customary lives.

From the beginning of the program up to January 15, 1935, the Bureau of Labor Statistics calculated that orders were placed for materials of the value of $701,315,937. The final stages, alone, of fabrication of these materials called for 2,296,543 man-months of labor, which is equivalent to the full employment of 127,586 men for eighteen months.

Orders for cement totaled more than 96 million dollars; for foundry and machine-shop products, more than 74 millions; for railway cars, more than 43 millions; for sand and gravel, nearly 45 millions; for lumber and timber products, more than 33 millions; for electric machinery and supplies, nearly 34 millions.

As the result of these orders additional men went back to work. In the car-building, electric and steam railroad industries, the number of men employed jumped from 15,680 in July of 1933, to 32,576 in July, 1934. Only 2,500 employees were on the rolls of firms manufacturing steam locomotives in July of 1933, but a year later nearly 7,000 men were employed, an increase of nearly 200 per cent.

The loans to railroads present an unusually good example of the indirect employment resulting from PWA. Practically the entire amount went to labor, yet only a small proportion was used for direct labor at the site. Most of the employment was in the shops of the railroads and in the mills and factories in which they placed orders. Materials and supplies used by the Pennsylvania Railroad in its electrification project, for instance, came from thirty-five States, spread across the continent from Connecticut to California. Approximately three thousand contracts with private industry were signed by the railroad officials.

The Bureau of Labor Statistics of the Department of Labor has found, with respect to labor put to work as a result of a loan for steel rails, that approximately four people are employed indirectly for every one who is at work on the site. The railroad companies, with loans from PWA, purchased in 1934 steel rails that provided 21 million man-hours of indirect industrial employment in all branches of the steel industry, in addition to 5 million 5 hundred thousand man-hours of employment for the railroad track forces that were called back to work to lay the rails.

PWA loans to nineteen railroads for rail purchases resulted in the manufacture of 424,744 tons in 1934, or 16,500 tons more than the total rail production of the steel industry in 1933. Purchases financed by PWA account for 1,007,746 tons or 42 per cent of the total rail production for 1934. This is an indication of what the PWA program has meant to the steel industry.

Every State in the Union has participated in the indirect employment furnished by PWA in proportion to the amount of construction materials they produce. Pennnsylvania and Ohio have received the greatest benefits because of their iron and steel, cement and clay products; Nevada and North Dakota have received the least but the former sold wall plaster and the latter concrete, clay and planing mill products.

To show the effect of this indirect employment on a town, I will cite the experience of Berwick, Pennsylvania. During the fourteen months' period from February 1, 1934 to March 31, 1935, the American Car and Foundry Company spent in its Berwick plant a total of $879,600 for wages in the execution of orders for which PWA was responsible.

This $879,600 represented approximately 55 per cent of the total payroll of the plant. At the peak of production on this work in August of 1934, 84 per cent of the total number of men employed were required to fill PWA orders. In this plant alone, the materials used during this period on PWA jobs amounted to more than 4 million dollars. A breakdown of this sum shows an interesting diversification of materials purchased and fabricated in different sections of the country:

Lumber	$ 190,500
Steel	902,550
Steel and Malleable Castings	117,050
Specialties	2,077,750
Air Brakes	242,200
Cast Iron and Steel Wheels	168,500
Springs	78,300
Paint	51,850
Other materials	232,300
Total	$4,061,000

It is no more possible to trace the final employment stimulated by money paid on a PWA construction project than it is for the eye to catch the last faint ripple resulting from the throwing of a stone into a quiet mill pond. The men employed directly at the site needed the materials fabricated at this Berwick plant. The men turning out this order in their turn required tools, power, supplies, fuel and oil. In order to supply these wants it was necessary to place orders in factories and mines in other localities and

States, resulting in increased employment there and in
stimulated business for idle industries. In all, the materials needed to operate the plant because of this PWA
order amounted to $267,500. In addition to the supplies
required by labor in order to fill the PWA order, the
workers in all the plants up and down the line that had
anything to do with supplying the goods, directly or indirectly, had more money to spend for food, clothing,
tobacco and amusements. Thus the ripples spread further
and further, each stimulating another with resulting additional employment, which in each case increased the
demand for consumer goods.

In addition to the quantity of employment made possible by PWA, standards of fairness to the worker have
been insisted on in all PWA projects. Since this program
was undertaken for the benefit of the unemployed we
have tried to safeguard their interests, to see to it that
they were given a square deal. We have scrupulously
followed the provisions laid down by Congress for a
thirty-hour week and a "just and reasonable wage" to
provide "a standard of living in decency and comfort."
We have insisted that every employer on a PWA project
provide adequate workmen's compensation insurance covering all labor employed by him if he could do so under
State law. In those States which do not have workmen's
compensation statutes, we have insisted on the best possible substitute.

Likewise, we have required that reasonable precautions
be taken at all times for the safety of the workers. We
even stipulated in our contracts that "all machinery and
equipment and other physical hazards shall be guarded in

accordance with the safety provisions of the manual of Accident Prevention in Construction of the Associated General Contractors of America, unless and to the extent that such provisions are incompatible with Federal, State or municipal laws or regulations."

To protect the workers against unfair wage practices we have insisted that all wage rates be posted prominently so that each worker could be sure that he was getting what he was supposed to get. We have also demanded that wages be paid in cash except in isolated places where, because of the hazards of carrying money, we have permitted payment by checks. Neither have we allowed any deductions from the payment of wages for commissary dues, premiums and the like, with the exception of certain premiums required by the laws of two States.

Throughout, we have striven for the best interests of the country, as well as for the welfare of the particular community served and of the workers employed. In my opinion these three objectives can be attained only if the interests of all are protected. PWA has constantly exerted its best efforts to that end.

Chapter XI

LOOKING BACKWARD

It was only natural that there should have been many conflicting ideas as to what PWA could or should do under the Act and much criticism of what it has done or failed to do. Everyone coming to PWA with a project, no matter how fantastic it might be, was always perfectly sure not only that it came within the Act but that the Act was drawn specifically to provide for that particular project. Also, as was to have been expected, some of the most enthusiastic supporters of the principle of public works in times of depression were sincere critics of PWA.

It soon came to be taken for granted that those who had the most to say in condemnation of PWA were the ones who had least cause for criticism, just as the man who summed up his feelings in the explosive expression "red tape" was likely to be the one who was himself dilatory beyond all patience or who was unable or unwilling to furnish essential information as the basis for our passing upon his project. Was a municipality behind in its tax collections, or in default on its bonds, or up to its borrowing limitation, failure to receive an allocation for a project was greeted with an indignant "red tape!" Did the constitution of a State prevent the borrowing of any money at all, State officials would cry "red tape," and hurry back home to tell their constituents that the Administrator of Public Works was a hardboiled, ill-mannered person who didn't know how to say anything except "No." Whether it was necessary to amend an ordinance, secure an enabling act or submit the question of issuing bonds to a referendum, PWA, in the eyes of the critics, was just inextricably wound about and in and out with "red tape."

It was puzzling to understand why such a storm of criticism and objurgation beat down upon our devoted heads until we began to analyze the situation. It was evident that many people believed that the Administrator not only was expected to perform a "loaves and fishes" miracle, but that he would promptly do so. The money had been voted by Congress, eager recipients were ready to receive their share of it and even a slight delay was exasperating and elicited an expression of impatient displeasure. Painstakingly, we had to explain over and over again, even to members of Congress who were responsible for the language of the Act, that so far as non-Federal projects were concerned, it was beyond our power to make loans unless the municipality that was the applicant for the loan could provide "reasonable security"; and even when this idea finally penetrated, city officials in many instances disingenuously offered "security" that was no security at all.

They tendered tax anticipation warrants at par when those warrants were a drug on the market because taxes were in arrears. They offered notes of hand or IOU's which they would not even have had the temerity to offer to a banker. When they had no "security" to tender they proposed in many instances that the United States Government put up a school building or dig a sewer and lease it to the community under a contract to amortize over a period of years, although the courts have held over and over again that such an indirect attempt to increase the debt of a municipality beyond its legal limits is in violation of the law.

Perhaps the most classic example of all arose in Chicago in connection with the outer bridge connecting the North and South Side boulevard systems at the mouth of the Chicago River. Money had been allocated for this project and then rescinded. The "security" offered in this instance was bonds issued for definite and specific purposes which had been redeemed at maturity, canceled and retired. The *Chicago Tribune,* in whose eyes this Administration can do nothing right and which would sneer and cavil at the Sermon on the Mount if thereby it could gain a partisan advantage, was especially savage in its denunciation of the Administrator because he would not do a "favor for his home city." In many instances there were such people who were perfectly willing that the Administrator should violate the plain intendment of the law as a special favor to themselves while insisting in the next breath that the PWA fund must be honestly and conservatively managed.

In time we became used to charges of "red tape" that were made when we failed to assure a municipality that we would ignore statutory or fundamental laws that the courts would not have permitted us to over-ride in any event even if we had sought to do so. We became accustomed to being damned for "slowness" because municipal authorities took from six months to a year to sign a contract, as happened in more than one instance; or because it was necessary to hold a referendum, or obtain enabling

SOURCE AND DISTRIBUTION OF PUBLIC WORKS FUNDS

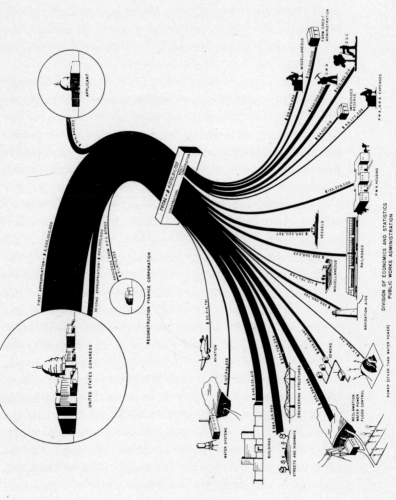

Chart showing sources and distribution of Public Works Funds as of April 1, 1935.

legislation. In course of time we became inured to being condemned for being "too strict."

Another type of criticism has become more vocal of late, criticism based on the proposition that PWA has been a failure because we are still in the depression and there remain millions of unemployed with no work to which to set their hands. Part of this criticism is honest, but a great deal of it is dishonest.

There are many who are frankly puzzled as to why the money allocated and expended by PWA has not had all of the results that they had persuaded themselves, or were led to believe, would flow from it. For such honest-minded critics, I think the situation can be clarified. The plain fact is that many people were too enthusiastic at the beginning about what the public works program would accomplish and the time within which it would do the accomplishing. Standing by itself, 3 billion 700 million dollars is undoubtedly a lot of money, but a simple comparison will demonstrate its total inadequacy from the point of view of what it was expected to do.

Experts differ as to the exact amount, but in the boom years of the decade prior to 1929 between 10 and 15 billions of dollars a year were expended in this country for improvements of the same general type that PWA was expected to finance. Now, no fair-minded man would expect the sum of 3 billion 700 million dollars, spread over two years, to be the same stimulus to business and industry as 10 or 15 billion dollars a year. Nor is this all of the story. Although the amounts of money available for public works up to April 1, 1935, have been approximately 3 billion 760 million dollars, only about $2,506,-

050,000 have been allocated for the 20,000-odd PWA construction projects. The remainder, or approximately 1 billion 200 million dollars,* went to CWA, CCC, TVA, the Farm Credit Administration and other recovery purposes. So, instead of having 3 billion 700 million dollars to expend over two years in comparison with the 10 to 15 billion dollars that went annually into construction prior to the depression, we have had only about two and one-half billions.

As the program grew in scope and our administrative machinery began to clank its way down the course that was set for it, conflicts of opinion became more frequent and sometimes more acute. We were called upon to resolve serious questions of labor policy involving wages, hours of work and conditions under which the work was to be performed. There were differences of opinion with State and municipal authorities over questions of jurisdiction; it became our duty to settle strikes; there were problems involving the interpretation, not only of the contracts under which the work was progressing, but of rules and regulations promulgated by us. What was the relationship of PWA to NRA? Did a contractor need to attorn to NRA before bidding or could he wait until the bids had been opened and then qualify for the contract? Would Negro labor have any rights at all, and if so, what were those rights and how could they be enforced? Such were typical instances of the acute controversial issues that kept arising constantly and calling not only for rare patience, but for keen judgment for their satisfactory solution.

* Cf. p. 40.

Nor have our relations with our applicants always been so smooth as we would have wished them to be. Occupied as our staff was with hundreds of projects from all corners of the land, and frequently overworked, we were not always able to render prompt service. At first we did not realize that the water system, which was only one of many projects to our examiners, was the big local issue for the mayor who wrote urgently demanding if it was going through. Nor could that particular mayor understand why his application was not put at the head of the list and the money asked for quickly granted.

When an application was received, it was announced. When an allotment was made, it was announced. When a contract was signed, it was announced. The philosophy behind our policy was that, dealing as we were with such tremendous forces, the Public Works Administration did not want to forego any benefit which might come from outside suggestions and suggestions could be intelligent only if outsiders knew what was being done. Also, in exploring new ground, PWA did not wish to dam up a tremendous backwater of errors which might loose destructive forces upon it. Such forces were already sufficiently potent without damming them up until they might burst bounds and wreck the program. So day by day, the story of the doings of PWA was told the country in a series of thousands of announcements.

A press section was established which has made public every completed action of PWA, while the Administrator has held press conferences twice a week at which he has submitted to searching cross-examination on every phase of the program by correspondents from every locality and reflecting every shade of opinion. Frequently, as many as sixty-five correspondents would question him and, when such examinations were over, there was little that was not of public record. At all times our theory was that the public was entitled to the fullest possible information and that is what we wanted it to have.

Of course there was "red tape," legal red tape and procedural red tape due to laws and customs that no one could cut through unless he were endowed with dictatorial powers over city councils, State legislatures, the comptroller general and the courts themselves. Of course the program was slow at times. No one was more impatient than was the Administrator at vexing delays that in most instances were absolutely unavoidable. Perhaps we were too strict on occasion and yet if there was even a reasonable doubt we always resolved it in favor of the applicant as can be shown in hundreds of cases.

That mistakes were made, I would be the last to deny. PWA has made mistakes, but we have always tried to keep our minds open and when our mistakes were brought home to us we let no pride of opinion stand in the way of correcting them. It may be admitted that PWA may make further mistakes, but if it does, I hope it will continue to have the courage to change its course when necessary to correct errors either of judgment or of action. If it is expected that a program of the magnitude and intricacy of PWA is to be administered without mistakes, then someone other than mere human beings must be found to entrust with its administration.

From the very beginning we were conscious of the desirability of speed and in the first flush of our enthusiasm we hurried to make loans to some twenty towns for desirable water and sewer facilities. Later some of these projects came back to plague us. I do not mean that we passed these without examination but we did accept too readily the optimistic estimates of the towns themselves. These things happened before we had set up engineers in the various States to conduct independent examinations.

This early attempt of ours to achieve speed furnishes a good example of the old adage that haste makes waste. One of the first projects approved at the beginning of my administration was on an application from a small town in Ohio. The town wanted to construct water and sewage systems and estimated that it would be able to get 200 customers for each service. As there was no doubt about the social desirability of these projects a loan and grant totaling $58,000 was made. The projects were completed by September of 1934, but eighteen months later there were only twenty-six water and just six sewer connections with little prospect of any more.

Instead of earning the $6,000 annual revenue predicted in the application, it now seems probable, on the basis of present receipts, that the yearly revenue will be $318. At the same time the cost of operation, instead of being $795 as promised in the application, will be, on the most favorable basis, approximately $2,100. There seems to be no way of making these two projects solvent despite the fact that the applicant definitely claimed they would be both "self-supporting" and "self-liquidating." Fortunately, such instances are rare. The ones referred to were worth the cost because they taught us to use greater care and to discount properly the claims of those asking for money.

It must be clear to everyone that if the majority of projects had been so mistaken as the one just described we might as well have taken our early analogy literally and dumped a million dollars at every milepost from Washington to San Francisco. There was enough money to do this and more. Those who think that the real purpose of PWA was to get money into circulation regardless of method would probably have been just as pleased with this plan as with any other, but this was never PWA's way of doing things. Moreover, I do not think it would have come even close to executing the mandate of Congress. What PWA sought to do was to get honest work at honest wages on honest projects, which was a great deal more difficult task than giving away money. I have leaned toward the theory that there are sufficient useful public works needed in this country so that no person should be employed doing useless work. PWA chose the harder course, and did so deliberately. It is still my belief that there is little to be gained in the long run from construction that cannot be economically justified.

Hundreds of thousands of projects flowed to the Public Works Administration and, in behalf of each of them, advocates could truthfully say "This will give employment." Most of them had to be rejected. The job of the Public Works Administrator rapidly developed into that of being the "No" man of Washington. I had to say "No" fifty times to every time I had an opportunity to say "Yes." In every governmental organization there is a tendency to refrain from making decisions, especially in hard cases, and pass them up the line. In the early days, it sometimes seemed to me that no one else in our organization would

accept the responsibility of saying "No." It is always un-
popular politically to say "No," while the "Yes" man is
the one who is loved. I undertook to inculcate into the
staff the belief that it is better in the long run to say "No"
as soon as the facts warrant it rather than to raise false
hopes by equivocation. Some persons felt that this was a
hard-boiled and negative attitude. I think it was an
honest one. However, certain objectors to the alleged slowness with which money has been spent have not and, in
my opinion, never will be satisfied. The theory of public
works as administered was sound but it has only a speaking acquaintance with the beliefs of those who considered
PWA primarily an agency to distribute money. Even those
who accepted the theory of public works as practiced by
PWA found much fault with the lack of speed of the
Administration. I have seen and heard PWA division
heads damn the obstacles which they encountered as they
sought to get projects under construction. I, myself, have
cursed these hindrances, but even when tempted to break
Federal, State or local laws to get work actually started,
I realized that any such short-cutting would not only
increase the difficulties in the long run, but would arouse
widespread dissatisfaction.

Slowest of all types of projects to reach the construction
stage were the non-Federal works—the schools, sewers,
water works, light plants and hospitals which, to my mind,
were the best projects of all. These projects first had to
be conceived and then worked out. It was surprising how
few of them were ready to be launched when the public
works program started. It was equally surprising how
many were planned after the program got under way.

When such a project was submitted to PWA, even after it was recognized that it was meritorious, weeks and sometimes months went by in accumulating the detailed information that it was necessary to have before action could be taken. Even vitally essential information was sometimes great in bulk and local officials were often slow in providing it. As soon as possible the allotment was made, frequently without waiting for all of the information, in the hope that the incentive of an allotment would speed up local action.

The layman, unfamiliar with the multitude of laws by which public expenditures and public construction are governed, carelessly characterizes these regulations as bureaucratic red tape and, frequently, I am tempted to join with him in this denunciation. But those who look closely will find something deeper than petty officialdom. Since the early days, public expenditures have been governed by increasing regulations put on the statute books for good and sufficient reasons. They were the expression of the bitter experience of the taxpayers during the years with wasteful, lavish and dishonest management of public funds. Behind each regulation, no matter how technical and small, there is understandable resentment against careless or faithless public officials. Also, most of these regulations were written on local statute books, with no idea of Federal coöperation on local public works, but they applied to the PWA program just as much as if the community affected had gone into the regular money marts to borrow money on its credit.

But, endless as these obstacles seemed to be, the staff managed to overcome them or get around them, and each time a new obstacle was encountered a new way out was discovered by those who were determined to drive the program through. Most of the barriers were of such a technical nature that the public at large never understood them or had interest to study them.

The staff of lawyers would draw contracts which had to conform to all local, State or national laws affecting these allotments. These agreements would be sent to the local officials and sometimes the project would seem to die at this point. It was all as new ground to the local officials as it was to the public works staff besides which they were afraid of the contracts and mystified by them. Frequently, they would go into some pigeonhole in a mayor's or governor's office and be lost. PWA men would take to the field, dig out the contracts and start them along their course once more, only to have them disappear again into some obscure corner.

Washington then would explain and plead with the various communities to get action and would also threaten to rescind the allotment. By and large, the threats were more effective than the pleadings but each threat brought down upon PWA a storm of criticism and recrimination which went unanswered. What we wanted was action and we were willing to accept the brickbats so long as we got action.

After the communities had executed the contracts and the government had signed in its turn, endless additional details were encountered. All the local regulations controlling public construction came into play to delay the actual start of work. Weeks became months and, in some instances, a year would pass before a non-Federal allotment resulted in construction which the public could watch. Yet during the entire period each project was continually being pushed by PWA.

Many municipalities which wanted to avail themselves of the opportunity of constructing useful utilities under the provisions of the Recovery Act found themselves entangled in a network of legal restrictions on their powers. For example, although the credit of Georgia and its cities stands as high as any, nevertheless constitutional limitations on the power to borrow money prevented the State and its municipalities from benefiting from our program on the same basis as many other borrowers.

While on the subject of Georgia, I want to refer to an experience which, fortunately, was rare, because generally speaking, practically all public officials with whom we have dealt in every part of the country have acted in the utmost good faith. This incident illustrates some of the difficulties which it was necessary for us to meet in our eagerness to give as widespread an effect as possible to the PWA program.

Yielding to the personal importunities of the governor of Georgia that some way be found to expend PWA money in his State in spite of constitutional limitations, some of our best lawyers spent literally months trying to devise a method to meet his wishes and our own desires. Finally we agreed, although against our better judgment, to build a much-needed State penitentiary and lease it back to the State under a contract that would provide for amortization and interest over a period of years. This was the most difficult, as certainly it was the most thankless, job that PWA has undertaken during its entire administration.

About the same time some of the counties of Georgia wanted funds with which to build roads. The only security they could offer consisted of non-interest bearing obligations of the State known as State of Georgia Highway Department Refunding Certificates. The opinion of our lawyers was that these certificates could not be pledged as security for PWA loans. Again the governor came to Washington to beg for special consideration, to demand favors that had not been extended to other communities. We pointed out that legislation would be necessary to cure certain defects in order to make these certificates valid security. The governor argued that his legislature was not in session and would not be until January of 1935. When it was suggested that a special session be called he objected on account of the expense involved.

Then, with the full knowledge and consent of Governor Talmadge of Georgia, a bill for a validating act was drawn with the approval of the attorney general of that State both as to form and substance. On June 5, 1934, the governor wrote me a letter in which he stated categorically that the bill as drawn, which had been submitted to him, would be recommended by him to the legislature when it convened in January of 1935. His letter closed with this paragraph: "I hope that you will have no further hesitation in making funds available to the various counties of the State of Georgia to which allotments have been made so that they may obtain the benefits of the National Industrial Recovery Act."

Relying on this solemn promise of a governor of a sovereign State, we made the allotments that he had pleaded for. When the Georgia legislature convened in 1935 Acting Deputy Administrator Fleming wrote to the governor enclosing a copy of the bill that had already been agreed upon and reminding him of his promise. The governor then began to evade and equivocate. He discovered reasons with which no lawyer could agree, why it was not necessary to pass the enabling act. He chose to ignore the suggestion that even if the act was not necessary, as he wrongly insisted, at least its passage would do no harm.

Finally, on March 16, when the matter was brought to my attention, I sent to the governor a long telegram urging action and concluding with this sentence: "Presence of this act on the statute books of the State, even though you think it is not necessary cannot in any way be prejudicial and would be evidence of your good faith." To this telegram I received no reply until long after the legislature had adjourned.

Now for the end of the story: The bill in question was passed by the legislature on March 22 and sent to the governor, who promptly vetoed it on March 28.

While we have had no similar experience with any other public official, even below the grade of governor, this illuminating incident will serve to justify the caution that we felt it was necessary to exercise in many instances in approving projects when we were asked to rely upon the promises of public officials instead of upon statutory authority. We early adopted the principle that these monies constituted trust funds that could not be whimsically administered, but must be carefully safeguarded under the law by every known administrative and contractual device.

As an example of a different sort, New York State

passed a statute declaring inoperative all laws which might interfere with the desires of municipalities to take advantage of the provisions of the National Industrial Recovery Act. However, this short cut proved the longest way around because the law was so ambiguous that it was useless. Nevertheless, the experience that we gained from such an effort as this proved of great help later when other States asked our advice on legal matters. For instance, when representatives of the State of New Mexico consulted PWA officials, a workable bill was quickly prepared for their use and was enacted into law at a special session.

Although in Georgia we urged the governor to keep his own written promises, quite properly PWA has never attempted to force States to pass any legislation. When requested by accredited representatives of the States, we have been only too glad to place the knowledge and experience of our legal staff at their disposal. But despite frequent requests from prominent persons in certain States, we have consistently refrained from endorsing or even recommending any special legislation that has been proposed, since we considered that this was a question to be decided by the State itself on the basis of its policy and its needs.

Whenever, at the request of a State, we have submitted to its governor a draft of a proposed law we have always suggested that it be given to the attorney general for possible revision in the light of the State's constitution. When a State legislature has amended a proposed law in accordance with local conditions, we have always considered such action entirely within its rights and duties.

In December of 1934, the President sent identical letters to governors of every State in the Union discussing legal policies. An extract from the one sent to Governor McAllister of Tennessee reads:

"In the event that an additional public works program is authorized at the coming session of the Congress, I should like to see the municipalities of your State legally able to take full advantage of such a program. With this in mind, I have instructed Administrator Ickes to place at your disposal the legal division of the Public Works Administration for the purpose of suggesting bills which if enacted into law would enable municipalities of your State to secure the benefits of this phase of the recovery program.

"Our experience in the past eighteen months has brought to light the difficulty of gearing the legal machinery which has served municipalities of your State adequately for decades to the speed with which the Federal Government must extend credit to achieve desired results. It has been found that revision of the procedure relative to municipal financing is essential, at least for the duration of the existing emergency."

As a result of these letters favorable replies were received from many of the States and at the specific request of those governors who asked for them, our legal division has supplied drafts of 487 bills to facilitate the participation of the States in the PWA program. In addition 76 bills have been supplied to private agencies which were confronted with legal difficulties in connection with their applications for loans.

This legal relationship is only one phase of the prob-

lem of the contacts between the Federal Administration
and States and municipalities. We have endeavored in
every possible way to make these relationships both
friendly and mutually beneficial. As I have indicated in
former chapters, we have been able to raise considerably
the standard of construction in many parts of the country.
Often we found that local people welcomed our efforts to
eliminate graft and curb corruption which, unaided, they
had been powerless to control. But even when we met
with resistance we insisted on straightforward dealings
and the carrying out of our contracts according to their
terms.

In many small towns from which applications came,
there had been in the past no effort to keep complete
financial records; the mere requirement that they should
fill out our questionnaires demanded more adequate accounting than they could supply. In such instances we
were glad to place at their service the more highly skilled
workers of our staff. We also called to their attention the
need for adequate coverage during construction, including
bonds against possible defaults by contractors, and the
commendable practice of requiring insurance on completed structures.

One other criticism was made of PWA during the national campaign of 1934. It was that funds entrusted to
us were used for political purposes in order to affect the
result of that campaign. This charge never had any basis
in fact and I am not even sure that it was made in good
faith; nevertheless, I will meet it.

PWA has never been in politics. It was not in politics
during the campaign referred to. Practically all of the

3 billion 300 million dollars originally appropriated was allocated by January 19 of 1934. On June 29 of the same year the additional 400 million dollars that has already been referred to was made over to us by order of the President. In anticipation of this new money, the PWA Board had previously, on June 20, approved 1,138 projects for a total of $153,565,000. From the time that this 400 million dollars was given to us, we allocated it as speedily as possible.

So fast did it go out that, as the political campaign progressed, we were approving fewer and fewer projects. The mighty stream of PWA funds had diminished to a mere trickle by midsummer of 1934. From that time on there was little money to appropriate for any project. Whereas it had been our practice to hold each week a meeting of the PWA Board for the purpose of passing on projects, during the three weeks immediately preceding the election not one such meeting was held. Not a single project was approved subsequent to October 17, 1934, until after the election on November 6, and not a future promise was made.

CHAPTER XII

THE JOB AHEAD

It cannot be disputed that much precious time was lost in getting the PWA program under way. This was inevitable considering the circumstances. There was no organization, no precedents, no plans. This Administration cannot justly be blamed for the lack of foresight on the part of its predecessors. We spend hundreds of millions of dollars annually to prepare us for war while at a cost of a comparatively few thousand dollars a year we could be prepared, at least in some measure, even for such a depression as the one through which we are now so painfully toiling. Preparedness for a period of depression is at least as important as preparedness for war. If we have learned no other lesson from our recent experience, it is to be hoped that at least there has been inculcated in us the firm resolve never again to be precipitated into an economic crisis without some plans and preparations kept up to date by a competent general staff of experts on planning.

Early in its existence, PWA, on the basis of its own experience, realized keenly the necessity for national planning on a broad scale. Accordingly we set up a National Planning Board to consider and develop a broad national plan of socially desirable public works. Naturally it was impossible for this board to formulate plans ahead of the work that it was so necessary to undertake. Adequate planning requires elaborate statistics based on research. These we did not have, nor did we have time to get them before embarking on our pressing job of providing employment quickly.

As a result, serious and unavoidable mistakes have been made. Later, when President Roosevelt created the National Resources Board, the National Planning Board was merged into and became the dominant factor in the larger body. Based on our experience, there is an unanswerable case for a permanent Federal agency to carry on the work so brilliantly begun by the National Planning Board so that there may be some assurance that there will not be a recurrence of the situation that confronted us when we were mustered in to fight the present depression. With a National Planning Board to serve as a general staff, there should be regional, State, and, in the larger and more important counties of the country, county planning boards, all coöperating with one another under the guidance of the Federal body.

During the decade beginning in 1920 public construction increased in volume until in 1930 it amounted to 3 billion dollars a year. This huge expenditure by municipalities, counties, States and the Federal Government constituted on an average through the period approximately one-quarter of the total construction bill in the country. This is a perfectly natural development, concomitant with the advance of civilization and the demand by an ever-growing proportion of the population for better social conveniences.

Although the Public Works Administration itself is an emergency agency born of the crisis, it is clear that it has merely taken over a job long recognized to be necessary. Our purpose has been to revive public construction to its normal level quite apart from the initiation of new developments in this field. After 1930 non-Federal governmental bodies found it increasingly difficult to finance their normal construction requirements and only PWA has enabled very necessary public works to be undertaken.

The question of the extent to which PWA in its present form should be called into operation in the future will depend upon the volume of private business; but it is important that we always be prepared to pick up the slack of idle labor and unused raw materials whenever the volume of private business decreases to an alarming degree.

Public works not only provides a way for using our labor and natural resources, it offers to the country an escape from the dilemma of the dole during a depression. To those who advocate adherence to so-called classical economic laws, even to the extent of letting the people perish, as well as to those who favor scattering Federal money as gifts, I say that the construction of useful and socially desirable public works is a much more sound and American solution of our difficulties.

With reference to the financing of public works, I confess my impatience with the argument that this Nation cannot afford useful public works, when the man power required to build those works would otherwise be wasted and unused. Public works which are useful give to the community something of enduring value, whether or not technically self-liquidating. Insofar as such works do not pay their way out of income or out of future savings which they make possible, they must be paid for out of taxes. Expenditures for public works are distributed among those who build the works and taxes are theoretically assessed proportionately against those who share in our national wealth. If economic activity dwindles, it becomes harder to pay taxes on our reduced income even though the rates are reduced. If business improves, it is easier to pay taxes on our increased income even if rates are raised. Work, not unemployment, creates wealth. It is the fashion for a certain group of pseudo-economists to dispose of public works with the glib remark that a nation must live within its income.

Many business men, especially those in the higher income tax brackets, as well as *laissez-faire* economists generally, have vigorously insisted during the past two years that unless we balance our budget we will soon find ourselves in irretrievable economic and political disaster. In the same breath they contend, and rightly, that in order to pull ourselves out of this depression we must give people who are able and willing to work an opportunity to work. To do this requires the investment of capital, particularly in the heavier industries. Now it happens that private capital for a long time has not shown the slightest disposition to seek employment in industry or in public works.

If we are to balance our budget, and that, according to these theorists, means that the government must not only be dependent upon current income for current expenditures, but may not draw on its credit even for funds to invest in permanent improvements (although it is recog-

The famous Washington Monument given a new face with a PWA
allotment of $100,000.

nized as being sound policy for private business to build permanent improvements out of surplus or from the sale of securities), then the Federal Government, which alone can step into this breach, will not be able to draw on its resources for the purpose of putting money into circulation. The reasoning seems to be along this line: business must be stimulated; only the investment of money can stimulate business; banks and private individuals possessing funds refuse to invest such funds; the Federal Government alone has both the money and the will to stimulate business; therefore, the government must *not* spend any money for this purpose, but, on the contrary, must keep strictly within its budget.

I agree that our budget cannot remain permanently unbalanced without disastrous results, but those who would balance it at once without regard to consequences seem to forget that if our national debt is particularly large at the present time it is so because the administrations during the prosperous years following the war adopted a policy of *tax* reduction rather than one of vigorous *debt* reduction. It should be kept in mind that about half of our national debt has been carried over from the war. Failure to reduce this indebtedness as rapidly as it could and should have been during the days of plenty appears to have been overlooked as one of the causes of a present unbalanced budget.

The budget balancers also ignore the fact that expenditures for capital improvements result in increasing the whole level of incomes, and therefore broadens the tax base, which is the foundation for treasury revenues. That this is true, there can be no doubt.

There are many other factors to be considered in this situation that are just as important as an immediate balancing of the budget. Not the least of these is the morale of the American people. To my way of thinking, it is more important in these times to preserve the morale of the people than it is to balance a set of books.

There is still another way of looking at this problem. The reservoir of money in the country must be tapped for life blood to infuse into the veins of industry in order to combat the pernicious anæmia from which it has been suffering. There are two sources through which this life blood can be obtained; one is private reserves and the other is the Federal treasury. If one source is clogged, then, if the patient is to be saved, the other outlet must be resorted to. After all, in theory, does it make a great deal of difference which faucet is turned on in order to get this money into circulation? It is the same money regardless of its depository. It is the wealth of America, the savings from the earnings of the workers of America.

Many billions of dollars could properly be spent in the United States on permanent improvements. Such spending would not only help us out of the depression, it would do much for the health, well-being and prosperity of the people. I refuse to believe that providing an adequate water supply for a municipality or putting in a sewage system is a wasteful expenditure of money. Any money spent in such fashion as to make our people healthier and happier human beings is not only a good social investment, it is sound from a strictly financial point of view. I can think of no better investment, for instance, than money paid out to provide education and to safeguard the health of

the people. Sound and well-trained minds in sound bodies
would add more to the actual prosperity of this country,
measured purely in money values, than anything I can
think of at the moment.

The government embarked on the public works program because of the timidity of private capital and its refusal to come out from under the bed. Something had
to be done about the depression if we were ever to shake
it off. And fortunately the great majority of the people
wanted to do something about it. They wanted to march
out and meet the enemy in hand-to-hand conflict. President Roosevelt had the same impulse, and immediately
after his inauguration he set out to engage in mortal combat as insidious and as relentless a foe as a champion has
ever faced.

Exponents of *laissez-faire,* as well as those who advocate the policy now being followed by this Administration
under the leadership of President Roosevelt, are in perfect agreement as to the necessity of a greater circulation
of our money resources if there is to be a business recovery. The New Deal, however, is not afraid to follow
through to the inevitable conclusion that if private capital
will not perform its functions, public capital must and
will. We will not adopt a defeatist attitude. We decline
to run away from logical facts. If the circulation of
money alone will restore health to the economic system
and only the Federal Government is able to provide that
money, then the Federal Government must and will
provide it.

[H. R. 5755]

AN ACT

To encourage national industrial recovery, to foster fair competition, and to provide for the construction of certain useful public works, and for other purposes.

Be it enacted by the Senate and House of Representatives of the United States of America in Congress assembled,

(TITLE I omitted)

TITLE II—PUBLIC WORKS AND CONSTRUCTION PROJECTS

FEDERAL EMERGENCY ADMINISTRATION OF PUBLIC WORKS

Section 201. (a) To effectuate the purposes of this title, the President is hereby authorized to create a Federal Emergency Administration of Public Works, all the powers of which shall be exercised by a Federal Emergency Administrator of Public Works (hereafter referred to as the "Administrator"), and to establish such agencies, to accept and utilize such voluntary and uncompensated services, to appoint, without regard to the civil service laws, such officers and employees, and to utilize such Federal officers and employees, and, with the consent of the State, such State and local officers and employees as he may find necessary, to prescribe their authorities, duties, responsibilities, and tenure, and, without regard to the

235

Classification Act of 1923, as amended, to fix the compensation of any officers and employees so appointed. The President may delegate any of his functions and powers under this title to such officers, agents, and employees as he may designate or appoint.

(b) The Administrator may, without regard to the civil service laws or the Classification Act of 1923, as amended, appoint and fix the compensation of such experts and such other officers and employees as are necessary to carry out the provisions of this title; and may make such expenditures (including expenditures for personal services and rent at the seat of government and elsewhere, for law books and books of reference, and for paper, printing and binding) as are necessary to carry out the provisions of this title.

(c) All such compensation, expenses, and allowances shall be paid out of funds made available by this Act.

(d) After the expiration of two years after the date of the enactment of this Act, or sooner if the President shall by proclamation or the Congress shall by joint resolution declare that the emergency recognized by section 1 has ended, the President shall not make any further loans or grants or enter upon any new construction under this title, and any agencies established hereunder shall cease to exist and any of their remaining functions shall be transferred to such departments of the Government as the President shall designate: *Provided,* That he may issue funds to a borrower under this title prior to January 23, 1939, under the terms of any agreement, or any commitment to bid upon or purchase bonds, entered into with such borrower prior to the date of termination, under this section, of the power of the President to make loans.

SEC. 202. The Administrator, under the direction of the President, shall prepare a comprehensive program of public works, which shall include among other things the following: (a) Construction, repair, and improvement of public highways and park ways, public buildings, and any publicly owned instrumentalities and facilities; (b) conservation and development of natural resources, including control, utilization, and purification of waters, prevention of soil or coastal erosion, development of water power, transmission of electrical energy, and construction of river and harbor improvements and flood control and also the construction of any river or drainage improvement required to perform or satisfy any obligation incurred by the United States through a treaty with a foreign Government heretofore ratified and to restore or develop for the use of any State or its citizens water taken from or denied to them by performance on the part of the United States of treaty obligations heretofore assumed: *Provided,* That no river or harbor improvements shall be carried out unless they shall have heretofore or hereafter been adopted by the Congress or recommended by the Chief of Engineers of the United States Army; (c) any projects of the character heretofore constructed or carried on either directly by public authority or with public aid to serve the interests of the general public; (d) construction, reconstruction, alteration, or repair under public regulation or control of low-cost housing and slum-clearance projects; (e) any project (other than those included in the foregoing classes) of any character heretofore eligible for loans under subsection (a) of section 201 of the Emergency Relief and Construction Act of 1932, as amended, and paragraph (3) of such subsection (a) shall for such purposes be held to include loans for the construction or completion of hospitals the operation of which is partly financed from public funds, and of reservoirs and pumping plants and for the construction of dry docks; and if in the opinion of the President it seems desirable, the construction of naval vessels within the terms and/or limits established by the London Naval Treaty of 1930 and of aircraft required therefor and construction of heavier-than-air aircraft and technical construction for the Army Air Corps and such Army housing projects as the President may approve, and provision of original equipment for the mechanization or motorization of such Army tactical units as he may designate: *Provided, however,* That in the event of an international agreement for the further limitation of armament, to which the United States is signatory, the President is hereby authorized and empowered to suspend, in whole or in part, any such naval or military construction or mechanization and motorization of Army units: *Provided further,* That this title shall not be applicable to public works under the jurisdiction or control of the Architect of the Capitol or of any commission or committee for which such Architect is the contracting and/or executive officer.

SEC. 203. (a) With a view to increasing employment quickly (while reasonably securing any loans made by the United States) the President is authorized and empowered, through the Administrator or through such other agencies as he may designate or create, (1) to construct, finance, or aid in the construction or financing of any public-works project included in the program prepared pursuant to section 202; (2) upon such terms as the President shall prescribe, to make grants to States, municipalities, or other public bodies for the construction, repair, or improvement of any such project, but no such grant shall be in excess of 30 per centum of the cost of the labor and materials employed upon such project; (3) to acquire by purchase, or by exercise of the power of eminent domain, any real or personal property in connection with the construction of any such project, and to sell any security acquired or any property so constructed or acquired or to lease any such property with or without the privilege of purchase: *Provided,* That all moneys received from any such sale or lease or the repayment of any loan shall be used to retire obligations issued pursuant to section 209 of this Act, in addition to any other moneys required to be used for such purpose; (4) to aid in the financing of such railroad maintenance and equipment as may be approved by the Interstate Commerce Commission as desirable for the improvement of transportation facilities; and (5) to advance, upon request of the Commission having jurisdiction of the project, the unappropriated balance of the sum authorized for carrying out the provisions of the Act entitled "An Act to provide for the construction and equipment of an annex to the Library of Congress," approved June 13, 1930 (46 Stat. 583); such advance to be expended under the direction of such Commission and in accordance with such Act: *Provided,* That in deciding to extend any aid or grant hereunder to any State, county or municipality the President may consider whether action is in process or in good faith assured therein reasonably designed to bring the ordinary current expenditures thereof within the prudently estimated revenues thereof. The provisions of this section and section 202 shall extend to public works in the several States, Hawaii, Alaska, the District of Columbia, Puerto Rico, the Canal Zone, and the Virgin Islands.

(b) All expenditures for authorized travel by officers and employees, including subsistence, required on account of any Federal public-works projects, shall be charged to the amounts allocated to such projects, notwithstanding any other provisions of law; and there is authorized to be employed such personal services in the District of Columbia and elsewhere as may be required to be engaged upon such work and to be in addition to employees otherwise provided for, the compensation of such additional personal services to be a charge against the funds made available for such construction work.

(c) In the acquisition of any land or site for the purposes of Federal public buildings and in the construction of such buildings provided for in this title, the provisions contained in sections 305 and 306 of the Emergency Relief and Construction Act of 1932, as amended, shall apply.

(d) The President, in his discretion, and under such terms as he may describe, may extend any of the benefits of this title to any State, county, or municipality notwithstanding any constitutional or legal restriction or limitation on the right or power of such State, county, or municipality to borrow money or incur indebtedness.

SEC. 204. (a) For the purpose of providing for emergency construction of public highways and related projects, the President is authorized to make grants to the highway departments of the several States in an amount not less than $400,-000,000, to be expended by such departments in accordance with the provisions of the Federal Highway Act, approved November 9, 1921, as amended and supplemented, except as provided in this title, as follows:

(1) For expenditure in emergency construction on the Federal aid highway system and extensions thereof into and through municipalities. The amount apportioned to any State under this paragraph may be used to pay all or any part of the cost of surveys, plans, and of highway and bridge construction including the elimination of hazards to highway traffic, such as the separation of grades at crossing, the reconstruction of existing railroad grade crossing structures, the relocation of highways to eliminate railroad crossings, the widening of narrow bridges and roadways, the building of footpaths, the replacement of unsafe bridges, the construction of routes to avoid congested areas, the construction of facilities to improve accessibility and the free flow of traffic, and the cost of any other construction that will provide safer traffic facilities or definitely eliminate existing hazards to pedestrian or vehicular traffic. No funds made available by this title shall be used for the acquisition of any land, right

of way, or easement in connection with any railroad grade elimination project.

(2) For expenditure in emergency construction on secondary or feeder roads to be agreed upon by the State highway departments and the Secretary of Agriculture: *Provided,* That the State or responsible political subdivision shall provide for the proper maintenance of said roads. Such grants shall be available for payment of the full cost of surveys, plans, improvement, and construction of secondary or feeder roads, on which projects shall be submitted by the State highway department and approved by the Secretary of Agriculture.

(b) Any amounts allocated by the President for grants under subsection (a) of this section shall be apportioned among the several States seven-eighths in accordance with the provisions of section 21 of the Federal Highway Act, approved November 9, 1921, as amended and supplemented (which Act is hereby further amended for the purposes of this title to include the District of Columbia), and one-eighth in the ratio which the population of each State bears to the total population of the United States, according to the latest decennial census and shall be available on July 1, 1933, and shall remain available until expended; but no part of the funds apportioned to any State need be matched by the State, and such funds may also be used in lieu of State funds to match unobligated balances of previous apportionments of regular Federal-aid appropriations.

(c) All contracts involving the expenditure of such grants shall contain provisions establishing minimum rates of wages, to be predetermined by the State highway department, which contractors shall pay to skilled and unskilled labor, and such minimum rates shall be stated in the invitation for bids and shall be included in proposals for bids for the work.

(d) In the expenditure of such amounts, the limitations in the Federal Highway Act, approved November 9, 1921, as amended and supplemented, upon highway construction, reconstruction, and bridges within municipalities and upon payments per mile which may be made from Federal funds, shall not apply.

(e) As used in this section the term "State" includes the Territory of Hawaii and the District of Columbia. The term "highway" as defined in the Federal Highway Act approved November 9, 1921, as amended and supplemented for the purposes of this section, shall be deemed to include such main parkways as may be designated by the State and approved by the Secretary of Agriculture as part of the Federal-aid highway system.

(f) Whenever, in connection with the construction of any highway project under this section or section 202 of this Act, it is necessary to acquire rights of way over or through any property or tracts of land owned and controlled by the Government of the United States, it shall be the duty of the proper official of the Government of the United States having control of such property or tracts of land with the approval of the President and the Attorney General of the United States, and without any expense whatsoever to the United States, to perform any acts and to execute any agreements necessary to grant the rights of way so required, but if at any time the land or the property the subject of the agreement shall cease to be used for the purposes of the highway, the title in and the jurisdiction over the land or property shall automatically revert to the Government of the United States and the agreement shall so provide.

(g) Hereafter in the administration of the Federal Highway Act, and Acts amendatory thereof or supplementary thereto, the first paragraph of section 9 of said Act shall not apply to publicly owned toll bridges or approaches thereto, operated by the highway department of any State, subject, however, to the condition that all tolls received from the operation of any such bridge, less the actual cost of operation and maintenance, shall be applied to the repayment of the cost of its construction or acquisition, and when the cost of its construction or acquisition shall have been repaid in full, such bridge thereafter shall be maintained and operated as a free bridge.

SEC. 205. (a) Not less than $50,000,000 of the amount made available by this Act shall be allotted for (A) national forest highways, (B) national forest roads, trails, bridges, and related projects, (C) national park roads and trails in national parks owned or authorized, (D) roads on Indian reservations, and (E) roads through public lands, to be expended in the same manner as provided in paragraph (2) of section 301 of the Emergency Relief and Construction Act of 1932, in the case of appropriations allocated for such purposes, respectively, in such section 301, to remain available until expended.

(b) The President may also allot funds made available by this Act for the construction, repair, and improvement of public highways in Alaska, the Canal Zone, Puerto Rico, and the Virgin Islands.

SEC. 206. All contracts let for construction projects and all loans and grants pursuant to this title shall contain such provisions as are necessary to insure (1) that no convict labor shall be employed on any such project; (2) that (except in executive, administrative, and supervisory positions), so far as practicable and feasible, no individual directly employed on any such project shall be permitted to work more than thirty hours in any one week; (3) that all employees shall be paid just and reasonable wages which shall be compensation sufficient to provide, for the hours of labor as limited, a standard of living in decency and comfort; (4) that in the employment of labor in connection with any such project, preference shall be given, where they are qualified, to ex-service men with dependents, and then in the following order: (A) To citizens of the United States and aliens who have declared their intention of becoming citizens, who are bona fide residents of the political subdivision and/or county in which the work is to be performed, and (B) to citizens of the United States and aliens who have declared their intention of becoming citizens, who are bona fide residents of the State, Territory, or district in which the work is to be performed: *Provided,* That these preferences shall apply only where such labor is available and qualified to perform the work to which the employment relates; and (5) that the maximum of human labor shall be used in lieu of machinery wherever practicable and consistent with sound economy and public advantage.

SEC. 207. (a) For the purpose of expediting the actual construction of public works contemplated by this title and to provide a means of financial assistance to persons under contract with the United States to perform such construction, the President is authorized and empowered, through the Administrator or through such other agencies as he may designate or create, to approve any assignment executed by any such contractor, with the written consent of the surety or sureties upon the penal bond executed in connection with his contract, to any national or State bank, or his claim against the United States, or any part of such claim, under such contract; and any assignment so approved shall be valid for all purposes, notwithstanding the provisions of sections 3737 and 3477 of the Revised Statutes, as amended.

(b) The funds received by a contractor under any advances made in consideration of any such assignment are hereby declared to be trust funds in the hands of such contractor to be first applied to the payment of claims of subcontractors, architects, engineers, surveyors, laborers, and material men in connection with the project, to the payment of premiums on the penal bond or bonds, and premiums accruing during the construction of such project on insurance policies taken in connection therewith. Any contractor and any officer, director, or agent of any such contractor, who applies, or consents to the application of, such funds for any other purpose and fails to pay any claim or premium hereinbefore mentioned, shall be deemed guilty of a misdemeanor and shall be punished by a fine of not more than $1,000 or by imprisonment for not more than one year, or by both such fine and imprisonment.

(c) Nothing in this section shall be considered as imposing upon the assignee any obligation to see to the proper application of the funds advanced by the assignee in consideration of such assignment.

SUBSISTENCE HOMESTEADS

SEC. 208. To provide for aiding the redistribution of the overbalance of population in industrial centers $25,000,000 is hereby made available to the President, to be used by him through such agencies as he may establish and under such regulations as he may make, for making loans for and otherwise aiding in the purchase of subsistence homesteads. The moneys collected as repayment of said loans shall constitute a revolving fund to be administered as directed by the President for the purposes of this section.

RULES AND REGULATIONS

SEC. 209. The President is authorized to prescribe such rules and regulations as may be necessary to carry out the purposes of this title, and any violation of any such rule or regulation shall be punishable by fine of not to exceed $500 or imprisonment not to exceed six months, or both.

ISSUE OF SECURITIES AND SINKING FUND

SEC. 210. (a) The Secretary of the Treasury is authorized to borrow, from time to time, under the Second Liberty Bond Act, as amended, such amounts as may be necessary to meet the expenditures authorized by this Act, or to refund any obligations previously issued under this section, and to issue therefor bonds, notes, certificates of indebtedness, or Treasury bills of the United States.

(b) For each fiscal year beginning with the fiscal year 1934 there is hereby appropriated, in addition to and as part of, the cumulative sinking fund provided by section 6 of the Victory Liberty Loan Act, as amended, out of any money in the Treasury not otherwise appropriated, for the purpose of such fund, an amount equal to $2\frac{1}{2}$ per centum of the aggregate amount of the expenditures made out of appropriations made or authorized under this Act as determined by the Secretary of the Treasury.

REËMPLOYMENT AND RELIEF TAXES

SEC. 211. (a) Effective as of the day following the date of the enactment of this Act, section 617 (a) of the Revenue Act of 1932 is amended by striking out "1 cent" and inserting in lieu thereof "$1\frac{1}{2}$ cents."

(b) Effective as of the day following the date of the enactment of this Act, section 617 (c) (2) of such Act is amended by adding at the end thereof a new sentence to read as follows: "As used in this paragraph the term 'benzol' does not include benzol sold for use otherwise than as a fuel for the propulsion of motor vehicles, motor boats, or airplanes, and otherwise than in the manufacture or production of such fuel."

SEC. 212. Titles IV and V of the Revenue Act of 1932 are amended by striking out "1934" wherever appearing therein and by inserting in lieu thereof "1935." Section 761 of the Revenue Act of 1932 is further amended by striking out "and on July 1, 1933" and inserting in lieu thereof "and on July 1, 1933, and on July 1, 1934,".

Sec. 213. (a) There is hereby imposed upon the receipt of dividends (required to be included in the gross income of the recipient under the provisions of the Revenue Act of 1932) by any person other than a domestic corporation, an excise tax equal to 5 per centum of the amount thereof, such tax to be deducted and withheld from such dividends by the payor corporation. The tax imposed by this section shall not apply to dividends declared before the date of the enactment of this Act.

(b) Every corporation required to deduct and withhold any tax under this section shall, on or before the last day of the month following the payment of the dividend, make return thereof and pay the tax to the collector of the district in which its principal place of business is located, or, if it has no principal place of business in the United States, to the collector at Baltimore, Maryland.

(c) Every such corporation is hereby made liable for such tax, and is hereby indemnified against the claims and demands of any person for the amount of any payment made in accordance with the provisions of this section.

(d) The provisions of sections 115, 771 to 774, inclusive, and 1111 of the Revenue Act of 1932 shall be applicable with respect to the tax imposed by this section.

(e) The taxes imposed by this section shall not apply to the dividends of any corporation enumerated in section 103 of the Revenue Act of 1932.

Sec. 214. Section 104 of the Revenue Act of 1932 is amended by striking out the words "the surtax" wherever occurring in such section and inserting in lieu thereof "any internal-revenue tax." The heading of such section is amended by striking out "surtaxes" and inserting in lieu thereof "internal-revenue taxes." Section 13(c) of such Act is amended by striking out "surtax" and inserting in lieu thereof "internal-revenue tax."

SEC. 215. (a) For each year ending June 30 there is hereby imposed upon every domestic corporation with respect to carrying on or doing business for any part of such year an excise tax of $1 for each $1,000 of the adjusted declared value of its capital stock.

(b) For each year ending June 30 there is hereby imposed upon every foreign corporation with respect to carrying on or doing business in the United States for any part of such year an excise tax equivalent to $1 for each $1,000 of the adjusted declared value of capital employed in the transaction of its business in the United States.

(c) The taxes imposed by this section shall not apply—

(1) to any corporation enumerated in section 103 of the Revenue Act of 1932;

(2) to any insurance company subject to the tax imposed by section 201 or 204 of such Act;

(3) to any domestic corporation in respect of the year ending June 30, 1933, if it did not carry on or do business during a part of the period from the date of the enactment of this Act to June 30, 1933, both dates inclusive; or

(4) to any foreign corporation in respect of the year ending June 30, 1933, if it did not carry on or do business in the United States during a part of the period from the date of the enactment of this Act to June 30, 1933, both dates inclusive.

(d) Every corporation liable for tax under this section shall make a return under oath within one month after the close of the year with respect to which such tax is imposed to the collector for the district in which is located its principal place of business or, if it has no principal place of business in the United States, then to the collector at Baltimore, Maryland. Such return shall contain such information and be made in such manner as the Commissioner with the approval of the Secretary may by regulations prescribe. The tax shall, without assessment by the Commissioner or notice from the collector, be due and payable to the collector before the expiration of the period for filing the return. If the tax is not paid when due, there shall be added as part of the tax interest at the rate of 1 per centum a month from the time when the tax became due until paid. All provisions of law (including penalties) applicable in respect of the taxes imposed by section 600 of the Revenue Act of 1926 shall, in so far as not inconsistent with this section, be applicable in respect of the taxes imposed by this section. The Commissioner may extend the time for making the returns and paying the taxes imposed by this section, under such rules and regulations as he may prescribe with the approval of the Secretary, but no such extension shall be for more than sixty days.

(e) Returns required to be filed for the purpose of the tax imposed by this section shall be open to inspection in the same manner, to the same extent, and subject to the same provisions of law, including penalties, as returns made under title II of the Revenue Act of 1926.

(f) For the first year ending June 30 in respect of which a tax is imposed by this section upon any corporation, the adjusted declared value shall be the value, as declared by the corporation in its first return under this section (which declaration of value cannot be amended), as of the close of its last income-tax taxable year ending at or prior to the close of the year for which the tax is imposed by this section (or as of the date of organization in the case of a corporation having no income-tax taxable year ending at or prior to the close of the year for which the tax is imposed by this section). For any subsequent year ending June 30, the adjusted declared value in the case of a domestic corporation shall be the original declared value plus (1) the cash and fair market value of property paid in for stock or shares, (2) paid-in surplus and contributions to capital, and (3) earnings and profits, and minus (A) the value of property distributed in liquidation to shareholders, (B) distributions of earnings and profits, and (C) deficits, whether operating or non-operating; each adjustment being made for the period from the date as of which the original declared value was declared to the close of its last income-tax taxable year ending at or prior to the close of the year for which the tax is imposed by this section. For any subsequent year ending June 30, the adjusted declared value in the case of a foreign corporation shall be the original declared value adjusted, in accordance with regulations prescribed by the Commissioner with the approval of the Secretary, to reflect increases or decreases (for the period specified in the preceding sentence) in the capital employed in the transaction of its business in the United States.

(g) The terms used in this section shall have the same meaning as when used in the Revenue Act of 1932.

SEC. 216. (a) There is hereby imposed upon the net income of every corporation, for each income-tax taxable year ending after the close of the first year in respect of which it is taxable under section 215, an excess-profits tax equivalent to 5 per centum of such portion of its net income for such income-tax taxable year as is in excess of $12\frac{1}{2}$ per centum of the adjusted declared value of its capital stock (or in the case of a foreign corporation the adjusted declared value of capital employed in the transaction of its business in the United States) as of the close of the preceding income-tax taxable year (or as of the date of organization if it had no preceding income-tax taxable year) determined as provided in section 215. The terms used in this section shall have the same meaning as when used in the Revenue Act of 1932.

(b) The tax imposed by this section shall be assessed, collected, and paid in the same manner, and shall be subject to the same provisions of law (including penalties), as the taxes imposed by title I of the Revenue Act of 1932.

SEC. 217. (a) The President shall proclaim the date of—

(1) the close of the first fiscal year ending June 30 of any year after the year 1933, during which the total receipts of the United States (excluding public-debt receipts) exceed its total expenditures (excluding public-debt expenditures other than those chargeable against such receipts), or

(2) the repeal of the eighteenth amendment to the Constitution,

whichever is the earlier.

(b) Effective as of the 1st day of the calendar year following the date so proclaimed section 617(a) of the Revenue Act of 1932, as amended, is amended by striking out "1½ cents" and inserting in lieu thereof "1 cent."

(c) The tax on dividends imposed by section 213 shall not apply to any dividends declared on or after the 1st day of the calendar year following the date so proclaimed.

(d) The capital-stock tax imposed by section 215 shall not apply to any taxpayer in respect of any year beginning on or after the 1st day of July following the date so proclaimed.

(e) The excess-profits tax imposed by section 216 shall not apply to any taxpayer in respect of any taxable year after its taxable year during which the date so proclaimed occurs.

Sec. 218. (a) Effective as of January 1, 1933, sections 117, 23(i), 169, 187, and 205 of the Revenue Act of 1932 are repealed.

(b) Effective as of January 1, 1933, section 23(r) (2) of the Revenue Act of 1932 is repealed.

(c) Effective as of January 1, 1933, section 23(r) (3) of the Revenue Act of 1932 is amended by striking out all after the word "Territory" and inserting a period.

(d) Effective as of January 1, 1933, section 182(a) of the Revenue Act of 1932 is amended by inserting at the end thereof a new sentence as follows: "No part of any loss disallowed to a partnership as a deduction by section 23(r) shall be allowed as a deduction to a member of such partnership in computing net income."

(e) Effective as of January 1, 1933, section 141(c) of the Revenue Act of 1932 is amended by striking out "except that for the taxable years 1932 and 1933 there shall be added to the rate of tax prescribed by sections 13(a), 201(b), and 204(a), a rate of three-fourths of 1 per centum" and inserting in lieu thereof the following: "except that for the taxable years 1932 and 1933 there shall be added to the rate of tax prescribed by sections 13(a), 201(b), and 204(a), a rate of three-fourths of 1 per centum and except that for the taxable years 1934 and 1935 there shall be added to the rate of tax prescribed by sections 13(a), 201(b), and 204(a), a rate of 1 per centum."

(f) No interest shall be assessed or collected for any period prior to September 15, 1933, upon such portion of any amount determined as a deficiency in income taxes as is attributable solely to the amendments made to the Revenue Act of 1932 by this section.

(g) In cases where the effect of this section is to require for a taxable year ending prior to June 30, 1933, the making of an income-tax return not otherwise required by law, the time for making the return and paying the tax shall be the same as if the return was for a fiscal year ending June 30, 1933.

(h) Section 55 of the Revenue Act of 1932 is amended by inserting before the period at the end thereof a semicolon and the following: "and all returns made under this Act after the date of enactment of the National Industrial Recovery Act shall constitute public records and shall be open to public examination and inspection to such extent as shall be authorized in rules and regulations promulgated by the President."

SEC. 219. Section 500 (a) (1) of the Revenue Act of 1926, as amended, is amended by striking out the period at the end of the second sentence thereof and inserting in lieu thereof a comma and the following: "except that no tax shall be imposed in the case of persons admitted free to any spoken play (not a mechanical reproduction), whether or not set to music or with musical parts or accompaniments, which is a consecutive narrative interpreted by a single set of characters, all necessary to the development of the plot, in two or more acts the performance consuming more than 1 hour and 45 minutes of time."

APPROPRIATION

SEC. 220. For the purposes of this Act, there is hereby authorized to be appropriated, out of any money in the Treasury not otherwise appropriated, the sum of $3,300,000,000. The President is authorized to allocate so much of said sum, not in excess of $100,000,000, as he may determine to be necessary for expenditures in carrying out the Agricultural Adjustment Act and the purposes, powers, and functions heretofore and hereafter conferred upon the Farm Credit Administration.

SEC. 221. Section 7 of the Agricultural Adjustment Act,

approved May 12, 1923, is amended by striking out all of its present terms and provisions and substituting therefor the following:

"Sec. 7. The Secretary shall sell the cotton held by him at his discretion, but subject to the foregoing provisions: *Provided,* That he shall dispose of all cotton held by him by March 1, 1936: *Provided further,* That, notwithstanding the provisions of section 6, the Secretary shall have authority to enter into option contracts with producers of cotton to sell to the producers such cotton held by him, in such amounts and at such prices and upon such terms and conditions as the Secretary may deem advisable, in combination with rental or benefit payments provided for in part 2 of this title.

"Notwithstanding any provisions of existing law, the Secretary of Agriculture may in the administration of the Agricultural Adjustment Act make public such information as he deems necessary in order to effectuate the purposes of such Act."

TITLE III — AMENDMENTS TO EMERGENCY RELIEF AND CONSTRUCTION ACT AND MISCELLANEOUS PROVISIONS

Section 301. After the expiration of ten days after the date upon which the Administrator has qualified and taken office, (1) no application shall be approved by the Reconstruction Finance Corporation under the provisions of subsection (a) of section 201 of the Emergency Relief and Construction Act of 1932, as amended, and (2) the Administrator shall have access to all applications, files, and records of the Reconstruction Finance Corporation relating to loans and contracts and the administration of funds under such subsection: *Provided,* That the Reconstruction Finance Corporation may issue funds to a borrower under such subsection (a) prior to January 23, 1939, under the terms of any agreement or any commitment to bid upon or purchase bonds entered into with such borrower pursuant to an application approved prior to the date of termination, under this section, of the power of the Reconstruction Finance Corporation to approve applications.

DECREASE OF BORROWING POWER OF RECONSTRUCTION FINANCE CORPORATION

SEC. 302. The amount of notes, debentures, bonds, or other such obligations which the Reconstruction Finance Corporation is authorized and empowered under section 9 of the Reconstruction Finance Corporation Act, as amended, to have outstanding at any one time is decreased by $400,-000,000.

SEPARABILITY CLAUSE

SEC. 303. If any provision of this Act, or the application thereof to any person or circumstances, is held invalid, the remainder of the Act, and the application of such provision to other persons or circumstances, shall not be affected thereby.

SHORT TITLE

SEC. 304. This Act may be cited as the "National Industrial Recovery Act."

Approved, June 16, 1933, 11:55 a.m.

APPENDIX B

MORE than 17,000 of PWA's 19,000 projects are completed or under construction and 109,600,000 man-weeks of employment have been already provided.

More than 11,500 projects are finished and in use and nearly 5,500 are under construction. Virtually all others are covered by contracts and ready for construction.

Over 2,000,000 persons have had jobs on construction sites, as shown by PWA payrolls. This does not include a vast amount of indirect "behind the lines" employment created by purchase of approximately $800,000,000 worth of materials.

Out of $3,760,000,000 of recovery funds, $2,560,000,000 went for 19,004 PWA construction projects. The remainder, approximately $1,200,000,000, was used for CWA, CCC, TVA, Farm Credit Administration and other recovery purposes.

Including dependents of those gainfully employed on construction sites and in material production and transportation, it is estimated that at least 10,000,000 persons have been directly benefited by expenditures to increase the national wealth through construction of useful public works as a substitute for direct relief.

In addition to the employment already created, the 5,500 projects now under construction plus the 2,000 on which construction will begin shortly will continue to provide a large amount of direct and indirect work.

Besides creating work, the public works program has provided employment for capital seeking investment opportunities. About $200,000,000 of bonds issued by municipalities and railroad companies to finance public works projects initiated by PWA already have been absorbed by the private investment market.

PWA has resold $57,000,000 of bonds purchased by it in making advances on non-federal loan and grant allotments. Recipients of combined loan and grant allotments for non-federal projects have sold to private investors $85,000,000 of bonds that PWA had agreed to purchase. It is estimated that municipalities which applied for grants only to cover 30 per cent of the cost of labor and materials on their projects have marketed about $40,000,000 of bonds to cover the remainder of the cost of their projects above the PWA grants.

The $57,000,000 of bonds purchased by PWA in making advances on loan and grant allotments and later resold have netted the government a profit of more than a million dollars. Sales are made to and through the Reconstruction Finance Corporation, in accord with PWA's practice of surrendering the duty of financing construction to the private investment market as that market is willing to resume the burden.

Federal projects being built by departments of the government have gone into construction more rapidly and provided more employment than the non-Federal projects for which PWA has made loans and grants to States, municipalities, and other types of public bodies. PWA allotted $1,559,-167,000 to government departments for 14,934 Federal projects and $747,575,000 in loans and grants to local public bodies for 4,040 non-Federal projects. In addition to these allotments to local public bodies, loans totalling $197,-126,500 were made to 30 railroad companies to create employment through property improvements and new equipment construction.

All but 520 of the 14,934 Federal projects were completed or under construction on April 1, 1935, 10,396 being finished and in use and 4,018 under construction. The projects under construction include huge dams, power plants and river and harbor improvements that will continue to provide employment for a year or so longer. A check of the status of non-Federal projects on that date showed that 1,163 had been completed and 1,444 were under construction.

The railroad improvement and construction program for which PWA loaned $197,126,500 to 30 railroad companies is over 75 per cent completed. Delivery has been made of most of the new cars and engines manufactured as a result of PWA efforts to revive the stagnant railway equipment business. Repairs to old cars and locomotives for which PWA made loans to create employment for railway shopmen are nearly finished. The Pennsylvania Railroad electrification project, the largest single railroad job, will be finished within a few months. Passenger trains are now operated electrically between New York and Washington and electrification of freight yards and terminals is proceeding rapidly.

PWA has put projects into 3,040 of the 3,073 counties of the Nation as well as into all of the territories and insular possessions from Hawaii to the Virgin Islands and from the Panama Canal Zone to Alaska. All PWA improvements are permanent additions to the national wealth.

As many of the projects are self-liquidating, more than $1,000,000,000 of the $2,700,000,000 allotted for their construction will be returned to the government. The government is protected by collateral on approximately three-fourths of the reimbursable amount.

Among the 1,163 completed non-Federal local improvements financed by PWA are 260 water systems, 235 street and highway jobs, 216 schools and 200 sewer and sewage disposal plant projects.

The 1,444 non-Federal projects under construction include 306 schools, 87 hospitals, 323 water systems, 233 sewer and sewage disposal plant projects and 133 street and highway jobs.

[H. J. Res. 117]

JOINT RESOLUTION

Making appropriations for relief purposes.

Resolved by the Senate and House of Representatives of the United States of America in Congress assembled, That in order to provide relief, work relief and to increase employment by providing for useful projects, there is hereby appropriated, out of any money in the Treasury not otherwise appropriated, to be used in the discretion and under the direction of the President, to be immediately available and to remain available until June 30, 1937, the sum of $4,000,000,-000, together with the separate funds established for particular areas by proclamation of the President pursuant to section 15 (f) of the Agricultural Adjustment Act (but any amounts thereof shall be available for use only for the area for which the fund was established); not exceeding $500,000,000 in the aggregate of any savings or unexpended balances in funds of the Reconstruction Finance Corporation; and not exceeding a total of $380,000,000 of such unexpended balances as the President may determine are not required for the purposes for which authorized, of the following appropriations, namely: The appropriation of $3,300,000,000 for national industrial recovery contained in the Fourth Deficiency Act, fiscal year 1933, approved June 16, 1933 (48 Stat. 274); the appropriation of $950,000,000 for emergency relief and civil works contained in the Act approved February

15, 1934 (48 Stat. 351); the appropriation of $899,675,000 for emergency relief and public works, and the appropriation of $525,000,000 to meet the emergency and necessity for relief in stricken agricultural areas, contained in the Emergency Appropriation Act, fiscal year 1935, approved June 19, 1934 (48 Stat. 1055); and any remainder of the unobligated moneys referred to in section 4 of the Act approved March 31, 1933 (48 Stat. 22): *Provided,* That except as to such part of the appropriation made herein as the President may deem necessary for continuing relief as authorized under the Federal Emergency Relief Act of 1933, as amended, or for restoring to the Federal Emergency Administration of Public Works any sums which after December 28, 1934, were, by order of the President impounded or transferred to the Federal Emergency Relief Administration from appropriations heretofore made available to such Federal Emergency Administration of Public Works (which restoration is hereby authorized), this appropriation shall be available for the following classes of projects, and the amounts to be used for each class shall not, except as hereinafter provided, exceed the respective amounts stated, namely: (a) Highways, roads, streets, and grade-crossing elimination, $800,000,000; (b) rural rehabilitation and relief in stricken agricultural areas, and water conservation, trans-mountain water diversion and irrigation and reclamation, $500,000,000; (c) rural electrification, $100,000,000; (d) housing, $450,000,000; (e) assistance for educational, professional and clerical persons, $300,000,000; (f) Civilian Conservation Corps, $600,000,000; (g) loans or grants, or both, for projects of States, Territories, Possessions, including subdivisions and agencies thereof, municipalities, and the District of Columbia, and self-liquidating projects of public bodies thereof, where, in the determination of the President, not less than twenty-five per centum of the loan or the grant, or the aggregate thereof, is to be expended for work under each particular project, $900,000,000; (h) sanitation, prevention of soil erosion, prevention of stream pollution, sea coast erosion, reforestation, forestation, flood control, rivers and harbors and miscellaneous projects, $350,-000,000: *Provided further,* That not to exceed 20 per centum of the amount herein appropriated may be used by the President to increase any one or more of the foregoing limitations if he finds it necessary to do so in order to effectuate the purpose of this joint resolution: *Provided further,* That no part of the appropriation made by this joint resolution shall be expended for munitions, warships, or military or naval matériel; but this proviso shall not be construed to prevent the use of such appropriation for new buildings, reconstruction of buildings and other improvements in military or naval reservations, posts, forts, camps, cemeteries, or fortified areas, or for projects for nonmilitary or nonnaval purposes in such places.

Except as hereinafter provided, all sums allocated from the appropriation made herein for the construction of public highways and other related projects (except within or adjacent to national forests, national parks, national parkways, or other Federal reservations) shall be apportioned by the Secretary of Agriculture in the manner provided by section 204 (b) of the National Industrial Recovery Act for expenditure by the State highway departments under the provisions of the Federal Highway Act of November 9, 1921, as amended and supplemented, and subject to the provisions of section 1 of the Act of June 18, 1934 (48 Stat. 993): *Provided,* That any amounts allocated from the appropriation made herein for the elimination of existing hazards to life at railroad grade crossings, including the separation or protection of grades at crossings, the reconstruction of existing railroad grade crossing structures, and the relocation of highways to eliminate grade crossings, shall be apportioned by the Secretary of Agriculture to the several States (including the Territory of Hawaii and the District of Columbia), one-half on population as shown by the latest decennial census, one-fourth on the mileage of the Federal-aid highway system as determined by the Secretary of Agriculture, and one-fourth on the railroad mileage as determined by the Interstate Commerce Commission, to be expended by the State highway departments under the provisions of the Federal Highway Act of November 9, 1921, as amended and supplemented, and subject to the provisions of section 1 of such Act of June 18, 1934 (48 Stat. 993); but no part of the funds apportioned to any State or Territory under this joint resolution for public highways and grade crossings need be matched by the State or Territory: *And provided further,* That the President may also allot funds made available by this joint resolution for the construction, repair, and improvement of public highways in Alaska, Puerto Rico, and the Virgin Islands, and money allocated under this joint resolution to relief agencies may be expended by such agencies for the construction and improvement of roads and streets: *Provided, however,* That the expenditure of funds from the appropriation made herein for the construction of public highways and other related projects shall be subject to such rules and regulations as the President may prescribe for carrying out this paragraph and preference in the employment of labor shall be given (except in executive, administrative, supervisory, and highly skilled positions) to persons receiving relief, where they are qualified, and the President is hereby authorized to predetermine for each State the hours of work and the rates of wages to be paid to skilled, intermediate, and unskilled labor engaged in such construction therein: *Provided further,* That rivers and harbors projects, reclamation projects (except the drilling of wells, development of springs and subsurface waters), and public buildings projects undertaken pursuant to the provisions of this joint resolution shall be carried out under the direction of the respective permanent Government departments or agencies now having jurisdiction of similar projects.

Funds made available by this joint resolution may be used, in the discretion of the President, for the purpose of making loans to finance, in whole or in part, the purchase of farm lands and necessary equipment by farmers, farm tenants, croppers, or farm laborers. Such loans shall be made on such terms as the President shall prescribe and shall be repaid in equal annual installments, or in such other manner as the President may determine.

Funds made available by this joint resolution may be used, in the discretion of the President for the administration of the Agricultural Adjustment Act, as amended, during the period of twelve months after the effective date of this joint resolution.

SEC. 2. The appropriation made herein shall be available for use only in the United States and its Territories and possessions. The provisions of the Act of February 15, 1934 (48 Stat. 351), relating to disability or death compensation and benefits shall apply to those persons receiving from the appropriation made herein, for services rendered as employees of the United States, security payments in accordance with schedules established by the President: *Provided,* That so much of the sum herein appropriated as the United States Employees' Compensation Commission, with the approval of the President, estimates and certifies to the Secretary of the Treasury will be necessary for the payment of such compensation and administrative expenses shall be set aside in a special fund to be administered by the Commission for such purposes; and after June 30, 1936, such special fund shall be available for these purposes annually in such amounts as may be specified therefor in the annual appropriation Acts. The provisions of section 3709 of the Revised Statutes (U. S. C., title 41, sec.

5) shall not apply to any purchase made or service procured in carrying out the provisions of this joint resolution when the aggregate amount involved is less than $300.

Sec. 3. In carrying out the provisions of this joint resolution the President may (a) authorize expenditures for contract stenographic reporting services; supplies and equipment; purchase and exchange of law books, books of reference, directories, periodicals, newspapers and press clippings; travel expenses, including the expense of attendance at meetings when specifically authorized; rental at the seat of government and elsewhere; purchase, operation, and maintenance of motor-propelled passenger-carrying vehicles; printing and binding; and such other expenses as he may determine necessary to the accomplishment of the objectives of this joint resolution; and (b) accept and utilize such voluntary and uncompensated services, appoint, without regard to the provisions of the civil-service laws, such officers and employees, and utilize such Federal officers and employees, and, with the consent of the State, such State and local officers and employees, as may be necessary, prescribe their authorities, duties, responsibilities, and tenure, and, without regard to the Classification Act of 1923, as amended, fix the compensation of any officers and employees so appointed.

Any Administrator or other officer, or the members of any central board, or other agency, named to have general supervision at the seat of Government over the program and work contemplated under the appropriation made in section 1 of this joint resolution and receiving a salary of $5,000 or more per annum from such appropriation, and any State or regional administrator receiving a salary of $5,000 or more per annum from such appropriation (except persons now serving as such under other law), shall be appointed by the President, by and with the advice and consent of the Senate: *Provided,* That the provisions of section 1761 of the Revised Statutes shall not apply to any such appointee and the salary of any person so apointed shall not be increased for a period of six months after confirmation.

Sec. 4. In carrying out the provisions of this joint resolution the President is authorized to establish and prescribe the duties and functions of necessary agencies within the Government.

Sec. 5. In carrying out the provisions of this joint resolution the President is authorized (within the limits of the appropriation made in section 1) to acquire, by purchase or by the power of eminent domain, any real property or any interest therein, and improve, develop, grant, sell, lease (with or without the privilege of purchasing), or otherwise dispose of any such property or interest therein.

Sec. 6. The President is authorized to prescribe such rules and regulations as may be necessary to carry out this joint resolution, and any willful violation of any such rule or regulation shall be punishable by fine of not to exceed $1,000.

Sec. 7. The President shall require to be paid such rates of pay for all persons engaged upon any project financed in whole or in part, through loans or otherwise, by funds appropriated by this joint resolution, as will in the discretion of the President accomplish the purposes of this joint resolution, and not affect adversely or otherwise tend to decrease the going rates of wages paid for work of a similar nature.

The President may fix different rates of wages for various types of work on any project, which rates need not be uniform throughout the United States: *Provided, however,* That whenever permanent buildings for the use of any department of the Government of the United States, or the District of Columbia, are to be constructed by funds appropriated by this joint resolution, the provisions of the Act of March 3, 1931 (U. S. C., Supp. VII, title 40, sec. 276a), shall apply but the rates of wages shall be determined in advance of any bidding thereon.

SEC. 8. Wherever practicable in the carrying out of the provisions of this joint resolution, full advantage shall be taken of the facilities of private enterprise.

SEC. 9. Any person who knowingly and with intent to defraud the United States makes any false statement in connection with any application for any project, employment, or relief aid under the provisions of this joint resolution, or diverts, or attempts to divert, or assists in diverting for the benefit of any person or persons not entitled thereto, any moneys appropriated by this joint resolution, or any services or real or personal property acquired thereunder, or who knowingly, by means of any fraud, force, threat, intimidation, or boycott, deprives any person of any of the benefits to which he may be entitled under the provisions of this joint resolution, or attempts so to do, or assists in so doing, shall be deemed guilty of a misdemeanor and shall be fined not more than $2,000 or imprisoned not more than one year, or both.

SEC. 10. Until June 30, 1936, or such earlier date as the President by proclamation may fix, the Federal Emergency Relief Act of 1933, as amended, is continued in full force and effect.

SEC. 11. No part of the funds herein appropriated shall be expended for the administrative expenses of any department, bureau, board, commission, or independent agency of the Government if such administrative expenses are ordinarily financed from annual appropriations, unless additional work is imposed thereupon by reason of this joint resolution.

SEC. 12. The Federal Emergency Administration of Public Works established under title II of the National Industrial Recovery Act is hereby continued until June 30, 1937, and is authorized to perform such of its functions under said Act and such functions under this joint resolution as may be authorized by the President. All sums appropriated to carry out the purposes of said Act shall be available until June 30, 1937. The President is authorized to sell any securities acquired under said Act or under this joint resolution and all moneys realized from such sales shall be available to the President, in addition to the sums heretofore appropriated under this joint resolution, for the making of further loans under said Act or under this joint resolution.

Sec. 13. (a) The acquisition of articles, materials, and supplies for the public use, with funds appropriated by this joint resolution, shall be subject to the provisions of section 2 of title III of the Treasury and Post Office Appropriation Act, fiscal year 1934; and all contracts let pursuant to the provisions of this joint resolution shall be subject to the provisions of section 3 of title III of such Act.

(b) Any allocation, grant, or other distribution of funds for any project, Federal or non-Federal, from the appropriation made by this joint resolution, shall contain stipulations which will provide for the application of title III of such Act to the acquisition of articles, materials and supplies for use in carrying out such project.

Sec. 14. The authority of the President under the provisions of the Act entitled "An Act for the relief of unemployment through the performance of useful public work, and for other purposes", approved March 31, 1933, as amended, is hereby continued to and including March 31, 1937.

Sec. 15. A report of the operations under this joint resolution shall be submitted to Congress before the 10th day of January in each of the next three regular sessions of Congress, which report shall include a statement of the expenditures made and obligations incurred, by classes and amounts.

Sec. 16. This joint resolution may be cited as the "Emergency Relief Appropriation Act of 1935."

Approved, April 8, 1935, 4 p. m.

INDEX

Abandoned Coal Mines, Pollution from, 168.
Accident Prevention, 206.
Acts
Black, 13.
Emergency Appropriation of 1934, 40.
Emergency Relief Appropriation Act of 1935, 260
Emergency Relief and Construction, 8.
Federal and Highway Act of 1916, 82.
National Industrial Recovery Act, 12, 19, 20, 23, 55, 56, 61, 83, 145, 221.
Public Works, 235.
R. F. C., 40.
Relief and Construction Act of 1932, 10.
Wagner-Peyser, 8, 31.
Advertising Club of New York, 9.
Agg, T. F., 85.
Aircraft carriers, 154.
Airports, 157
Alcatraz Prison, 77.
All-American canal, 112.
Allen, Geo. G., 142.
American Car and Foundry Company, 204.
American Construction Council, 4, 7.
American Expeditionary Forces, 17.
American Federation of Labor, 9, 10, 31.
American Institute of Architects, 18.
American Society of Civil Engineers, 11, 17, 20.
Approval of Allotments, 68.
Arkansas river, 110.

Associated General Contractors of America, 207.
Atlanta, Ga., 190.
Atterbury, Gen. W. W., 152.
Aviation maps, 158.

Balanced budget, 231.
Ballinger scandals, 60.
Bangor and Aroostook Railroad, 59.
Baruch, Bernard M., 9.
Battle, Turner W., 23, 24.
Bauer, Carl, 75.
Bayside high school, 91.
Beck, James M., 15.
Bell, Daniel W., 24.
Benton, Philip M., 59.
Berwick, Pa., 204.
Bibles, 19.
Biggs, Solicitor General J. Crawford, 23, 24, 42, 43.
Birmingham, Ala., 120.
Black Bill (the), 13.
Black Canyon, 111.
Board of Labor Review, 34, 76.
Board of Review, 71.
Boise, Idaho, 110.
Bonneville dam, 107, 119, 125.
Border inspection stations, 162.
Boulder Canyon, 110, 112.
Boulder City, 114.
Boulder dam, 112, 118, 125.
Bricklayers', Masons', and Plasterers' International Union of America, 32.
Brigham City, 105.
Brookhart, Smith W., 10, 11.
Brownlow, Louis, 52.
Bubonic plague, 169.
Building Trades Depts., A. F. of L., 32.

Macmillan 9-12-35